STUDIES IN ECONOMIC AND SOCIAL HISTORY

This series, specially commissioned by the Economic History Society, provides a guide to the current interpretations of the key themes of economic and social history in which advances have recently been made or in which there has been significant debate.

Originally entitled 'Studies in Economic History', in 1974 the series had its scope extended to include topics in social history, and the new series title, 'Studies in Economic and Social History', signalises this development.

The series gives readers access to the best work done, helps them to draw their own conclusions in major fields of study, and by means of the critical bibliography in each book guides them in the selection of further reading. The aim is to provide a spring-board to further work rather than a set of pre-packaged conclusions or short-cuts.

ECONOMIC HISTORY SOCIETY

The Economic History Society, which numbers over 3000 members, publishes the *Economic History Review* four times a year (free to members) and holds an annual conference. Enquiries about membership should be addressed to the Assistant Secretary, Economic History Society, Peterhouse, Cambridge. Full-time students may join the Society at special rates.

GW00673426

STUDIES IN ECONOMIC AND SOCIAL HISTORY

Edited for the Economic History Society by T. C. Smout

PUBLISHED

OTHER TITLES ARE IN PREPARATION

British Rule
and the Indian Economy
1800–1914

Prepared for
The Economic History Society by

NEIL CHARLESWORTH

Lecturer in Economic History
University of Glasgow

First published 1982 by
THE MACMILLAN PRESS LTD
London and Basingstoke
Companies and representatives throughout the world

ISBN 0 333 27966 2

Phototypeset by
VANTAGE PHOTOTYPESETTING CO LTD
Southampton and London

Printed in Hong Kong

Contents

To Sarah, Fiona and Laura

Notes on References

References in the text within brackets refer to the numbered items in the Select Bibliography, followed, where necessary, by the page numbers in italics, for example [13: *78*]. The other references, numbered consecutively, relate to the items specified in the Notes and References section.

Editor's Preface

SINCE 1968, when the Economic History Society and Macmillan published the first of the 'Studies in Economic and Social History', the series has established itself as a major teaching tool in universities, colleges and schools, and as a familiar landmark in serious bookshops throughout the country. A great deal of the credit for this must go to the wise leadership of its first editor, Professor M. W. Flinn, who retired at the end of 1977. The books tend to be bigger now than they were originally, and inevitably more expensive; but they have continued to provide information in modest compass at a reasonable price by the standards of modern academic publication.

There is no intention of departing from the principles of the first decade. Each book aims to survey findings and discussion in an important field of economic or social history that has been the subject of recent lively debate. It is meant as an introduction for readers who are not themselves professional researchers but who want to know what the discussion is all about – students, teachers and others generally interested in the subject. The authors, rather than either taking a strongly partisan line or suppressing their own critical faculties, set out the arguments and the problems as fairly as they can, and attempt a critical summary and explanation of them from their own judgement. The discipline now embraces so wide a field in the study of the human past that it would be inappropriate for each book to follow an identical plan, but all volumes will normally contain an extensive descriptive bibliography.

The series is not meant to provide all the answers but to help readers to see the problems clearly enough to form their own conclusions. We shall never agree in history, but the discipline will be well served if we know what we are disagreeing about, and why.

T. C. SMOUT
Editor

University of St Andrews

Introduction

OVER the past twenty years, detailed research on the economic history of India in the British period has extended considerably, greatly increasing our knowledge of the subject. Whilst the work will continue – the publication of the *Cambridge Economic History of India* (edited by Dharma Kumar), promised soon, forms a major example – this seems an appropriate time to review the broad themes under discussion and make some preliminary judgements. In this essay, I have attempted to do this for the period 1800–1914. Detailed statistical material (available in the works referred to) has been deliberately excluded in order to highlight the general analysis.

As always, in such a work, one incurs wide debts to those with particular specialisms, and I am very grateful indeed to friends and colleagues who freely provided advice, especially Clive Dewey, Forbes Munro, Richard Saville and B. R. Tomlinson. I also greatly valued the help and encouragement of Professor Eric Stokes, given not long before his untimely death in February 1981. I, of course, am solely responsible for the work's conclusions and deficiencies. Mrs Blythe O'Driscoll and Mrs Linda Craig efficiently typed the text and my wife, Sarah, acted throughout as unpaid assistant and secretary. To her, and to our daughters, I owe a special debt.

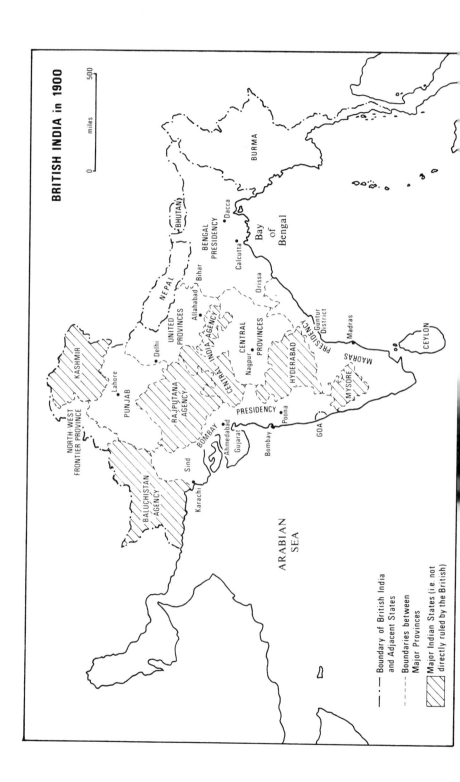

1   The Nature of the Debates

INDIA'S economic history in the nineteenth century demands attention at two levels. At one, there are the developmental problems experienced historically by an important and populous less developed country, characterised in 1800 by typically low levels of output but possessing a tradition of high-quality handicraft production and merchant enterprise. However, India also presents the classic case study of the effects of formal imperialism on a non-Western economy and society. Not only did British imperial rule last longer here than in any other major territorial possession but its impact was apparently more intrusive. The nature of revenue raising, for example, in which land revenue, paid by landlord or peasant, provided the major source of government income throughout the nineteenth century demanded – unlike the colonial fiscal forms of Africa or the Dutch East Indies – detailed definition and continuous knowledge of the village social structure and patterns of landownership.

These characteristics early established, in contemporary writings about the Indian economy, assumptions about the all-powerful nature of British rule. Marx commented in the 1850s that 'England has broken down the entire framework of Indian society' [5: 90]. Nevertheless, mirroring mid nineteenth-century attitudes, he expected an imminent Indian industrial revolution to arise from the ruins, predicting that 'the railway system will . . . become, in India, truly the forerunner of modern industry' [5: 136]. It was the disappointment of these hopes over the last third of the nineteenth century which first created an articulate critical literature. Modern industries, it is true, were by now developing, but their impact remained limited, vastly outweighed by the immense agricultural sector where famine seemed more rather than less persistent. Were, then, the conditions of British rule acting to prevent a fully fledged industrial revolution? Naoroji highlighted an alleged 'drain' of wealth from India to pay the 'home charges' for defence and

11

administration and to service debts to foreign investors [1]. Others, like Dutt and Digby, emphasised the burden of land taxation on agriculture and the subversion of India to British imperial needs, evident in the absence of tariff protection and a government purchasing policy which stimulated British rather than Indian industry [2;3].

At the same time, emerging fitfully from the apologia of administrators, another interpretation of events developed. On the assumption, again, that imperial rule had revolutionary effects, some major innovations seemed indisputably advantageous: the imposition of political unity and administrative efficiency and the construction of an elaborate infrastructure which, by 1914, included large irrigation schemes and the most extensive rail network in Asia. British rule, on the argument of such as Griffiths [4], was a powerful, positive force for modernisation. If the process of industrialisation remained sluggish, then the backwardness of the traditional economy and its slow reaction to developmental impulses determined this.

This established framework of discussion has been of great value to the subject. The contemporary debate provides the earliest and still one of the most direct formalisations of what is clearly the central issue of the Third World's modern history: whether, and in what ways, relations with the advanced, industrialised world have promoted or handicapped development. The traditional battleground remains frequently fought over in the modern literature. Thus when M. D. Morris was rash enough, in the early 1960s, to stress the positive features of India's development in the nineteenth century [13: *ch. 1*], he was set upon by three critics [13: *chs 2, 3, 4*], one of whom denounced the article as containing 'hardly a proposition . . . which (Sir) John Strachey, Lord Curzon etc, have not earlier put forward' [13: *37n*]. In practice this was unfair since the symposium and much subsequent work represents, as we shall see, considerable refinement of traditional arguments, but the statement accurately reflected the nature of the disagreement.

Paradoxically, however, the existence of this 'great tradition' of Indian economic history has not always helped to popularise the subject. The debates have been concerned primarily with the direct effects of formal imperialism. The 'drain' argument, for example, was about estimating the running costs of the imperial connection and, in contemporary accounts, agitating for reform [130], not any conceptual explanation of the relationship between a developed country and its imperial possession. This empirical tradition has remained prominent within the literature and, as a result, the recent broad controversial constructs evolved to explain the history of regions of informal empire like Latin America, but adapted and applied also within Africa – dependency, 'the development of underdevelopment'[1] – found few echoes in writing on India. However, economic historians of India, even if the thunder of theoretical debate frequently passed over them, have compiled considerable detail about the sub-continent's evolution. Thus India now provides not only an important case in its own right but a valuable test for wider hypotheses. India's prominent role in the nineteenth-century world also underpins this. If, for example, the Third World was 'underdeveloped' through its financial and commercial interchange with the West, then the phenomenon should have been especially striking in India, since she was, as we shall see, a central pillar of the nineteenth-century international trade economy.

How, though, has the modern literature refined traditional debates? The issue of whether British rule was fundamentally beneficial or harmful will always stay open, since the answer partly depends on counterfactual assessment of the alternatives. The cases of China and Japan suggest radically differing possibilities of what might have happened if India, like them, had remained politically independent. Recently, however, interpretations have developed which strongly question the all-powerful nature of imperialism. The thesis first emerged from studies of the land, where works like Frykenberg's examination of one Madras district revealed the British land systems, for all their superficially impressive formalism, as at root *ad hoc* and often ineffectual compromises with local reality [61]. Similar arguments have since been applied to the economy. Tomlinson, for example, comments of the indigenous financial system that 'the impact of a growing international market for Indian produce . . . helped to strengthen traditional agencies, rather than cause a breakdown' [138: *10*]. On this interpretation, imperialism, even in India, was too weak to transform economy and society. Its impact had simply a distorting effect since the provision merely of external stimuli actually bolstered pre-modern structures and attitudes. This line of argument essentially returns the prime mover behind economic and social development to traditional indigenous forces, reasserting the twofold nature of enquiry within Indian economic history which we established at the beginning.

In gauging the imperial impact, too, questions of the scale of importance of different sectors arise. One might demonstrate, for example, that Britain's commercial relationship with India was highly 'exploitative', but the significance of that factor as an impediment to Indian development would still partly depend on the prominence of the foreign trade sector within the Indian economy.

These preliminaries established, some further general points can be made. The first is a warning that in writing about India we are discussing a massive amalgamation of intensely varying regional and local circumstance. Even politically, British control was not all-embracing, for the princely states, which were never formally annexed, covered approximately one third of the sub-continent's area.[2] In India, any generalisation will risk contradiction in the locality.

This said, some broad comment is undoubtedly possible on the nature of the pre-British economy. Eighteenth-century India was not sunk in some primeval 'Asiatic' stagnation. Some of its handicraft production of textiles, notably the muslins of Dacca, was sold widely for export, and in commercial centres like the western port of Surat wealthy merchant groups existed. Perhaps India's fundamental problem, however, was the small-scale nature of most internal markets: 'largely a cluster of village economies', as Matsui describes the economy of 1800 [13: 19]. This meant that merchant enterprise and capital and credit resources remained cramped within isolated confines, so that there was no opportunity for the spontaneous emergence of a broadly based commercial and industrial expansion and the infrastructure necessary to support it. Equally fundamental, seventeenth and eighteenth-century India achieved only fitfully the political and social stability secured by the *Pax Tokugawa* in Japan; and the British conquest, involving sixty years of major warfare after 1757 and subsequent mopping-up operations, exacerbated this problem [13: 89]. In sum, the sub-continent in 1800 was undoubtedly far from any spontaneous industrial take-off.

Nevertheless, as Raychaudhuri remarks [13: 78], this was no reason why considerable growth and change should not have occurred by 1914. Some societies, notably Russia, achieved substantial industrial development during the nineteenth century from a highly backward base, fundamentally through import of Western techniques and capital. India as the leading imperial possession of the foremost capitalist nation should have been well placed to achieve this. In practice, of course, modern industrialisation did steadily develop during the second half of the nineteenth century, pioneered by the Bombay cotton industry and the Calcutta jute industry. It seems likely now, too, that claims made by Morris for significant increases in per capita production over the nineteenth century are justified [13: *ch. 1*], although this may amount to mere recovery from eighteenth-century decline [13: *90*]. Quantitative assessments of national income cannot be conclusive for the nineteenth century where statistical inadequacies, particularly on agriculture, are considerable; but Mukherjee's careful account suggests a rise of about 18 per cent in real per capita national income between 1860 and 1900 [22: *64*].

On this basis, one might reasonably argue that India's economic development between 1800 and 1914 represented a solid achievement, granted the obstacles and the relatively low level at the base. Equally, however, the process can be seen as both unreasonably sluggish and essentially flawed in nature. Assessment of per capita performance, for example, says nothing about distribution, which may have been sufficiently distorted to reduce the living standards of many; Bhatia's claims for 'a disconcerting increase' in famine frequency during the nineteenth century might suggest this [42]. Modern industry's performance, too, faced strict limitations. The cotton industry, for instance, did not win substantial control over the home market until the 1930s and then only through a retrenchment operation under protection following the loss of yarn export markets to Japanese competition.

Before examining such specific issues, however, we require some understanding of the basic chronological framework. Before 1850, one might argue, the stimulus of British commercial and industrial capitalism on the Indian economy was limited or at least sectorally variant. For the handicraft producer, as we shall see, the competition of manufactured imports may have presented a sharp shock, but within the country modern factory industry did not begin operations until the 1850s. To Marx, of course, this signalled the destructive waste-laying operation, but the scale of the foreign trade sector was at this stage probably small, and commercially India's greatest significance as a trading partner for Britain would only emerge as British industry came under serious challenge from competitors during the late nineteenth century. Analysis of modern business activity, therefore, will necessarily concentrate largely on the period after 1850.

This itself, though, illustrates the priorities of early British rule. The main constructive impact of the early nineteenth century came with social and legal reform, reflecting the Utilitarian assumption

15

that improvement and modernisation would follow judicial enactment [131]. At another level, however, the British were simply 'the latest of the predatory conquerors of Asia' [66: 45]. In this vein, following the plundering activities of the early nabobs, the fundamental concern was the creation of an efficient and pliant administrative structure and, particularly, the mobilisation of the financial resources to pay for British rule. This latter function, pursued relentlessly, did unquestionably represent a crushing imperial impact on the grass-roots economy. The Bombay territories, for example, acquired in 1818, were yielding double their then total for land revenue within four years [2: 65]. By the year of Victoria's accession, total land revenues received by the British authorities stood at nearly £12 million, rising thereafter to £17.7 million by 1857 [2: 212].

This inflow of funds depended, however, on the development of land revenue systems and detailed 'settlements', inquiries adjudicating on levels of assessment. This in turn necessitated important decisions on tenure and proprietary rights, for land had to have recognised owners to yield revenue. In every way, then, the most direct initial impact of British rule came on the land and with revenue policy – the issue we must, therefore, first examine.

2   The Land and Agriculture

(i) THE IMPACT OF BRITISH LAND POLICY

BY the middle years of the nineteenth century the land revenue systems and consequent tenurial structure throughout British India exhibited a pattern of striking provincial variation. The large Bengal Presidency, the first great territorial acquisition, boasted a *zamindari* system, in which the British had conferred rights of revenue payment and landlord and magisterial status on the *zamindar* overlords. Throughout most of the south and west 'however' – in the Bombay and Madras Presidencies – revenue settlements had attempted to break through to the actual cultivators of the soil, ensuring a *ryotwari* or peasant proprietary tenure. In the later acquisitions of the Punjab, the North-west Provinces and finally Oudh, a hybrid system of *mahalwari* settlements was widespread – here effective ownership of most land was vested in cultivators but land revenue was rendered communally by the village.

What, though, had been the impact of these different systems? One obvious interpretation is that they represented primarily the social and political preconceptions of British officialdom imposed in the face of, and therefore disrupting, traditional Indian arrangements; Cornwallis's *zamindari* settlement of 1793 in Bengal, for example, seemed to owe much to late eighteenth-century Whiggish regard for gentry proprietorship [59]. The dominance of such attitudes was, however, short-lived, soon to be challenged by the rise of Utilitarianism in the early nineteenth century. Stokes has argued, in a well-known study [131], that ideological distaste for landlordism, born of Utilitarian philosophy, was a major force behind the development of the *ryotwari* and *mahalwari* settlements, with the implication that policy may have ruined traditionally powerful landlord groups. Possible examples here are the *taluqdars* of northern India, whose previous control over the revenue settlements of many villages was frequently set aside by *mahalwari* arrangements. In particular, the undermining of the Oudh *taluqdars*, following

17

Dalhousie's annexation of the kingdom in 1856, undoubtedly stimulated support within Oudh for the great Mutiny uprising of 1857–8, a situation acknowledged by Canning's subsequent restitution of *taluqdari* rights [62].

There is little doubt that some prominent revenue officials, like Robert Bird [131: *115*], were driven by political ideology to diminish established landlord rights. The existence of such attitudes, however, merely raises the question, now widely posed, as to how powerful British policy actually could be on the ground. The British were not acting upon a passive agrarian society, and their revenue systems, as described in the official documents, are often, arguably, formalisations of arrangements which necessarily were much more flexible and pragmatic in the village. In the strictest *ryotwari* system, it was sometimes difficult to recognise the appropriate level of cultivating right and any indigenous élites, in practice, were probably able to preserve extensive powers in many villages. Frykenberg's picture of one Madras district's 'system' is of a desperate and often highly inefficient quest for revenue, necessarily making allowances for a mass of local social variations [61]. Even at overall provincial level, it might be argued, the basic structure of indigenous land tenure dictated the broad shape of local governments' policies. Munro seemed to turn first to *ryotwari* arrangements in early nineteenth-century Madras because he simply could not discover here the allodial gentry which the continuation of the Cornwallis Bengal policy required [60: *80*].

The whole discussion, however, is complicated by this very fact that official ideology and local reality often did not act as antitheses. In the minds of such as Munro and Wingate – the leading figures behind respectively the Madras and Bombay systems – Utilitarian dislike of landlordism was doubtless reinforced by practical experience of regions where cultivating peasants typically controlled the land. This correlation, though, would suggest that the British land systems were not, generally, revolutionary instruments of change. Certainly even the formal flexibility of the provincial systems is striking; within them, there was room for major variations like the settlement with small proprietors in Midnapur District of *zamindari* Bengal and the acceptance of overlord rights in the Konkan and Gujarat regions of *ryotwari* Bombay [66: *32*].

In practice, British land revenue policies may have been most disruptive, not through their adjudication of land tenure, but at the simple level of financial demands they made. Many of the early

18

British settlements – notably the 'Permanent Settlement' of Bengal of 1793 and Pringle's in Bombay during the 1820s and 1830s – were marked by considerable overassessment. The British, in their zeal for funds, often accepted the most optimistic inherited estimates of agriculture's capacity to pay, claims which were excessive in the depressed conditions of the first third of the nineteenth century. As a result, many proprietors were unable to meet the demands and were either driven into debt and dispossession or found their lands directly sold up for revenue arrears. In Bengal, titles to more than a third of the land apparently changed hands in the twenty-two years following the Permanent Settlement [64: 29], and in Banaras Province of northern India official documents speak of the transfer of nearly half the land in the years 1801–6 alone [63: 69].

Undoubtedly, then, the inauguration of the British land settlements typically stimulated a high turnover of land. However, the overall impact on agrarian social structure may have been limited. Individuals clearly rose and fell but most modern district studies have suggested that the complexion of landholding, viewed by social and caste group, did not shift radically. In Cohn's Banaras, for example, whilst many of the beneficiaries were 'in some senses . . . new men' [63: 78], the traditionally dominant caste groups – Rajputs, Brahmans and Bhumihars – still provided 67 per cent of landed proprietors in 1885 [63: 88]. The situation was clearly similar in Bengal where 'many of the land transfers were made to relatives, dependents and former employees of the old zamindars' [64: 29]. In addition, any assessment of change created by British settlements needs to recognise that the eighteenth century probably witnessed considerable turnover in land rights. In this vein, McLane characterises the Permanent Settlement's effects as 'less a revolution than a failure to end a continuing revolution or turnover among the ranks of superior landholders' [64: 19]. Nevertheless, the tendency, as British rule proceeded, was arguably for land revenue's disruptive effects to diminish. Already before 1850, revenue demands were being reduced sharply in many districts, the product not only of guilt about overassessment but of recognition that the stimulus to agriculture thus provided often boosted, through the creation of new taxable holdings, overall revenue receipts. Finally, in terms of political consequences, Stokes's recent work has undermined the notion of the Mutiny conflagration of 1857–8 as a simple outburst by the victims of British policy [66: chs 5–8]. The pattern of agrarian disturbances was complex and local economic factors, such as relative agricultural performance, were often more important than the impact of revenue settlements.

All this is not to deny the existence of change in Indian rural society during the first half of the nineteenth century. For a man like Tikam Singh of Mursan, Oudh, who was deprived of two-thirds of his ancestral estates [62: 77], the impact of the British land settlements could not be called inconsequential. Nevertheless, change was more often in individual status than in the substance of agrarian society.

(ii) AGRICULTURE AND POPULATION

This discussion of land revenue and its impact, in turn, takes us to the fundamental question of the actual performance of agriculture, since reliable revenue supply depended at root on this. Indeed, detailed assessment of India's whole economic development in the nineteenth century must focus strongly on the agricultural sector, for it was overwhelmingly both the largest employer of labour and the greatest single contributor to GNP. The 1901 Census enumerated over 65 per cent of the Indian population as directly dependent on agriculture[3] and many of the remainder serviced the agricultural economy as handicraft workers, labourers, shopkeepers and traders. Recognising this, many would conclude with Macpherson that 'the failure of agriculture to improve faster provided a serious, perhaps the most serious hindrance to development' [14:157].

Undoubtedly Indian agriculture faced severe problems throughout the nineteenth century, for even Morris concedes that 'the condition of the agriculturist . . . was grim' [31: 192]. Like other regions of monsoon Asia, India was traditionally characterised by fairly dense settlement relative to land availability, particularly in the Ganges Plain and Bengal. However, the great Asian agricultural achievement of high-yielding rice cultivation – Braudel's 'miracle of the paddy fields'[4] – was in India fully established only in these most populous regions of the north and east. Over much of peninsular India millet grains and pulses, more adaptable to unfavourable conditions but less high-yielding and potentially dynamic, predominated; they covered nearly half of the acreage devoted to foodgrains in 1900. At the same time, Indian agriculture typically shared the obvious disability of Asian rice economies, the limited importance of the livestock sector. There was a relatively large cattle population but of generally poor quality and its dung was typically used as fuel rather than as manure. Even millet cultivation, too, was heavily dependent on rainfall, which varied substantially from locality to locality, year to year and even decade to decade. Over the Bombay Presidency, for instance, average rainfall between 1898 and 1906 was apparently 20 per cent lower than in 1886–97, with much more dramatic slumps in individual years [44: *145*]. Shortfalls in production, in such circumstances, were inevitable.

These, however, were traditional difficulties. What is important to investigate is the progressive trend in agricultural performance during our period. For much of the nineteenth century definitive evidence is badly lacking; comprehensive statistics on crop acreage and output only exist from the last years of the century. Nevertheless, George Blyn's working of these figures presents firm conclusions for the period after 1891 [26]. They suggest, generalising for all crops and all provinces, some small expansion in per capita output during the 1890s, soon overtaken, however, by a major watershed during the early twentieth century when extending population growth began to press on means of subsistence. After 1911–12 down to Independence, Blyn estimates, overall per capita output in Indian agriculture was declining at a rate of 0·72 per cent per year. Blyn's calculations, then, may lend some support to Morris's assumptions of rising per capita production in the nineteenth century, but, if Blyn is right, the gains were inconsequential, already being overturned in many regions by 1914.

But is Blyn right? Recently, powerful doubts have been raised. Like Ohkawa and Rosovsky in Meiji Japan, Blyn fundamentally took the official statistics at face value and as in Japan, critics have, in turn, sought to expose the deficiencies of statistics, basically compiled as a waste product of the land revenue collection system. Dewey points to the sheer inaccuracy of much of the statistic gathering procedure [27]. It rested at root on the returns of the mass of often illiterate and corruptible village officials or, occasionally, on sporadic and often unrepresentative crop-cutting experiments. In addition, bias was introduced by attempts to evade land revenue, a bias which crucially, as in Japan, was subject to a distinct historical evolution. In Meiji Japan the government's ability to prevent land tax evasion and enforce statistical accuracy was notably less in the 1870s than in the 1910s. Hence the earlier statistics more greatly underestimate harvest performance than the later, in turn exaggerating (to what extent remains a matter of dispute) the rate of growth of agricultural production in between.[5] In India, arguably, this historical process was reversed. As Heston shows for Bombay [28], local administration, thanks to growing pressure of nationalist agrarian protest, was less powerful and effective on the ground by the 1920s and 1930s compared with forty years previously. District officials mollified tensions by providing the pessimistic estimates of local agricultural performance which would moderate land taxation demands; but these same estimates were reflected in the agricultural statistics which Blyn faithfully collated. Blyn's story of watershed and then decline may therefore be substantially a reflection of these developments. In sum, the changing agricultural output statistics, as they stand, possibly tell us as much about the shifting authority of local administration as about actual agricultural performance.[6] Subtle and detailed examination of the statistics at provincial and local level might still yield dividends, as Islam's recent study of Bengal [35] suggests. As yet, however, the nettle has rarely been grasped.

We seem, then, to be thrown back largely upon deduction from the broad general indicators. Despite the absence of full national census data before the 1870s, it is clear that overall population was rising steadily. Morris estimates an increase in the sub-continent's total population from just under 200 million in 1800 to over 285 million by 1901 [41], whilst Das Gupta's equivalent figures for the modern state of India – 154 million rising to 237 million [40: *435*] – suggest a slightly faster growth rate. Even the latter, however, amounting to about 0.4 per cent per annum, was not rapid by contemporary international standards and, further, this figure remained the rate of increase, recorded in the censuses, for the half century after 1871 [43: *640*]. Could agricultural production match or even exceed this? The technology of peasant farming certainly experienced no substantial change: in 1951 wooden ploughs apparently outnumbered iron ones by a factor of more than thirty to one [13: *49*]. Lack of capital gravely inhibited the use of fertiliser and government attempts to spread improved seed and better farming techniques achieved minimal impact. Official efforts had much their greatest effect in the field of irrigation with the provision of large canal schemes in the Punjab and parts of the United Provinces. Most localities, however, remained entirely dependent on traditional sources of water supply.

Nevertheless, there were other ways of increasing agricultural production. The likelihood is that the cultivated acreage throughout much of India grew substantially over the nineteenth century, particularly during its middle third [32: *ch. 1*]. By 1850 agriculture seems generally to have been recovering rapidly from its earlier trough and the lessening of revenue demands may have helped to stimulate the extension of cultivation. Mostly the expansion was the outcome of innumerable small clearing operations by peasants, but there were also some spectacular regional examples. Assam, for instance, was sparsely populated and largely jungle when annexed by the British in 1826; by 1902, following Guha's 'big push', over four million acres were under cultivation, particularly in tea plantations [37]. Gauging the overall scale of the expansion is clearly difficult, again raising questions of statistical accuracy, but official figures on acreage are, arguably, less susceptible to error and manipulation than those for output, particularly when studied at provincial and regional level. Recent assessments of later periods – of the Central Provinces between 1872 and 1921 [38] and of Bombay Presidency in the period 1900–20 [36] – suggest that, even then, the rate of expansion of cultivation was fully matching that of population.

However, deduction about agricultural performance remains complex even in these cases. The demographic evidence itself is equivocal. Population expanded enough to suggest an increased capacity within the system to support higher numbers, but its relatively low overall growth rate was undoubtedly mainly the outcome of periodic crisis. There were frequent famines, particularly serious in the late 1870s and late 1890s. Klein argues that in northern India 'population stability . . . did not imply favourable economic conditions but, simply, the hardship Indians faced' [34: *193*]; average life expectancy did not exceed twenty-five years until after 1921 [39: *36*]. Also, the characteristic that slow overall population growth was not an even process, but substantially the product of occasional severe bouts of high mortality, has obvious implications for population/land ratios. At times, like the 1880s and early 1890s, population was apparently growing rapidly and intense pressure on land resources could have built up in some areas. This, further, raises the obvious question whether the newly cultivated land was not of poorer quality and markedly lower productivity. In any case, rapid expansions in cultivation could create problems; more land, for example, demanded more widespread tillage but, in turn, the cattle which pulled the ploughs lived off the very grazing land which might be threatened by extension of cultivation. Where, as in early twentieth-century western India, the necessary response was greatly increased cultivation of specific 'fodder crops' [36: *121*], that clearly acted as a limitation on the value of the expansionary process.

Land in India, then, was not super-abundant. For the peasantry the expanding frontier of cultivation could never act as a 'safety valve' for development, because the spectacular occurrences, as in Assam, were under the control of European planter interests and the extensions in land available to peasants were more closely linked to population demand. The peasant, too, faced constant threats of disease and death. Even mortality rates, however, are not necessarily decisive indicators of economic trends. Japan experienced severe famine during the 1830s, barely half a century before modern economic growth is characterised as beginning, and slow population growth which crises like this created over the late Tokugawa period is often now seen as a developmental advantage.[7] From the initial evidence of population and land, we must think it likely that per capita agricultural production rose perceptibly in India between 1800 and 1914.

But this says nothing about the nature of production, which, arguably, changed considerably during the nineteenth century. A wide range of commercial crops extended acreage rapidly and, as a result, nineteenth-century India became a major exporter of raw cotton, rice, opium, wheat and tea and the monopolist producer of raw jute. These six crops contributed over 60 per cent of India's total exports in 1890 and, as we shall see later, exports were sufficient to maintain a substantial surplus on merchandise trade. In some ways, then, here was genuine agricultural revolution. The land revenue, too, remained the government's major single source of taxation throughout the nineteenth century, still providing over a quarter of total revenue and receipts in the 1890s. Perhaps such a contribution was necessary from a sector so dominant within the overall economy. Nevertheless, by the test of surplus benefits made available to the economy as a whole – the test often applied to agriculture's role in more rapidly developing economies like eighteenth-century Britain or Meiji Japan – agriculture in nineteenth-century India was not a stagnant force.

However, the character, extent and effects of commercialisation in the village raises complex questions. At one level, cash crop agriculture brought self-evident benefits. The trend in output performance was almost certainly more buoyant than in foodgrain production [26;35;14: *137*] and, at times, the export crops enjoyed large windfall price increases. Although in India, as elsewhere, there is debate whether the peasant cultivator was predominantly concerned with income maximisation or family consumption needs [68], a basic responsiveness to such commercial opportunities has now been conclusively demonstrated, particularly by Harnetty's description of the dramatic impact on cotton cultivation of the American Civil War price explosion [45], Narain's review of the crop acreage/price relationship over the early twentieth century [46] and Islam's account of twentieth-century Bengal [35]. Besides such price incentives, communications improvement, notably the opening of railways, acted to stimulate and reward commercial producers by cutting transport costs [56]. However, commercialisation of the rural economy proceeded in an irregular, diversified manner. Transport improvement by-passed large areas, like the Konkan region of western India [53: 113]. Cash crops often required special, rarely obtainable conditions; extensive water supply for sugar-cane production, for example. This all intensified regional and local disparities in both the nature and performance of agriculture. Where, as in parts of the United Provinces and the Deccan, new irrigation facilities were carved out from within an arid subsistence agriculture, the resulting dualism was especially striking.

Most important, did the expansion in commercial agriculture typically endanger the peasantry's supply of foodgrains? In general, since cultivated acreage was rising, cash crop expansion probably created absolute decline in acreage under foodgrains in only isolated, localised instances, and recent studies suggest that the peasantry's price-responsiveness was flexible enough to protect its own subsistence needs [35;49: 683]. Further, there was no inevitable separation and conflict between 'foodgrain' and 'commercial' production, since cultivation of the different crops sometimes complemented one another, as Chaudhuri comments of jute and rice cultivation in Bengal [55: 250–1]. Against this, demanding crops like cotton and sugar-cane certainly may have driven the foodgrains from the better quality land, with consequent threat to output performance. Again, technical innovations may have had ecological cost. Whitcombe argues that canal irrigation in northern India eventually created disadvantages such as waterlogging and the formation of saline deposits on the soil [50], though it remains likely, as Stone has demonstrated for one district [51], that the balance of advantage still favoured the canals, particularly so in the Punjab.

The usual assumption is that the costs associated with commercialisation fell disproportionately on the poorer peasants. They were often driven to the market to supplement their food supplies and some were enmeshed in dependent relationships created by their economic and caste status [74]. However, even for them, as McAlpin has claimed in a series of powerful revisionist tilts [47;48;49], the process of commercialisation may have brought some advantages, particularly by offering wider employment opportunities. Crops like cotton and jute, compared with the foodgrains, were relatively labour-intensive and their cultivation probably created part-time jobs for small landholders as well as additional employment for landless labourers. McAlpin suggests that extension of commercial agriculture in some regions may even have created local labour shortages by 1900, in turn driving up real wages for labour employment [48].

McAlpin's determinedly meliorist viewpoint has recently been applied, also, to the famine problem. In western India, she argues, unusually deficient rainfall was the major cause of the late nineteenth-century disasters and from 1900 a more flexible agricultural economy, coupled with a more efficient governmental response, limited the threat of serious mortality [44]. Certainly the evidence of famine is by no means clear-cut. Greater incidence in the nineteenth century may be partly the product of more thorough knowledge and reportage. Again, the long-term trend, as McAlpin comments, was to be favourable: 'from 1908 to 1942', Bhatia concedes, 'India experienced . . . no major famine involving any considerable loss of life' [42: *309*]. Nevertheless, this might suggest that the famines of the late nineteenth century were the product of a particular stage in India's economic evolution. The advent of railways, for example, with their accompanying sharp boost to exports, may have led to the depletion of grain stocks, traditionally preserved as an insurance against famine. It seems likely that in the first stages of commercialisation – before the advantages McAlpin delineates would be available – poor peasants were especially vulnerable to bad harvests.

Of course, any general comment about the nature and performance of agriculture is subject to massive provincial, regional and local variation. Indeed, as research proceeds at these levels, diversity is emerging as perhaps the fundamental theme of India's nineteenth-century agricultural history. The Punjab, with the special advantage of extensive irrigation, seems to have been the pacemaker, for, even on Blyn's figures, per capita output of all crops increased here by nearly 45 per cent between 1891 and 1921 [26:

26

122]. At the other extreme stood Bengal, where agriculture seemed to be facing genuine crisis by the early twentieth century, despite demands made upon it by a population growth faster and more sustained than elsewhere in India. At this stage gross cultivated acreage was apparently even declining, whilst population increase totalled over 10 per cent between the Censuses of 1901 and 1921 [33: *248*]. Thereafter, Islam's story is of only minimal improvement in aggregate yields and extent of cultivation between 1920 and 1946, despite the continuation of rapid population growth down to the famine of 1943 [35]. Similarly, Bihar and Orissa seems to have been in a highly unfavourable situation, at least by the twentieth century [35: *16*]. In most other provinces agricultural trends were probably less violent. In the Central Provinces, for example, some slight increase in per capita output is the most likely deduction from a situation where expansion of the area under foodgrains steadily matched the growth in population between 1860 and 1920 [38]. Even provincial assessments, however, represent broad generalisation: the pattern of disparity was repeated at much lower levels. Within the Bombay Presidency, for instance, agricultural performance seemed, in the long run, much more buoyant in Gujarat than further south, with the coastal region of the Konkan a particular laggard [36: *123–4*].

How, then, can we summarise so complex a picture? Nothing we have said has denied the belief that productivity was always comparatively low in Indian agriculture and that this may have been consistently the fundamental barrier to development. Nevertheless, the progressive trend in the nineteenth century was far from uniformly stagnant. Agriculture provided the major support for foreign trade and government revenue. It created pacemaking areas, where production experienced striking growth and diversification. In this sense agriculture in our period was firmly participating in India's development.

For all the attacks on Blyn's statistics, however, it still seems likely that the per capita expansion of the nineteenth century experienced reversal in many provinces – although not the Punjab – at some point during the early twentieth century. The era from around the middle of the nineteenth century down into the 1890s was the high period of agricultural development in British India, but by the 1920s there was more rapid and consistent population growth on the land and in some areas – notably in Islam's Bengal [35] – an equilibrium of stagnation was being reached, where cultivated acreage and yields had encountered tight constrictions on their expansion. Even where conditions were more buoyant the inter-war depression may have provided a powerful body blow against commercial agriculture. Some, indeed, now see the poor harvests and famines of the late 1890s as a watershed; Harnetty claims that wheat export from the Central Provinces never recovered from this setback [38]. If this is so, the force of the nineteenth-century expansionary thrust was decisively weakening at the very moment when, on McAlpin's interpretation, distributionary problems associated with its development were beginning to be ameliorated. Doubts, then, must remain over agriculture's performance at every historical point. Nevertheless, our review perhaps suggests that its role as an impediment to India's development in the nineteenth century may have been exaggerated.

(iii) SOCIAL STRUCTURE AND AGRARIAN CHANGE, 1850–1914

At this point, however, we must return to questions of social structure and change. For the impact of the land revenue systems forms merely a precursor of the possible social changes on the land wrought by British rule; after 1850 the development of a more commercialised agricultural economy raised the spectre of more. Many Indian peasants, for example, were constantly in debt – often to finance agricultural operations as well as special needs such as wedding celebrations – to other peasants, overlord groups or to village moneylenders and traders. During the second half of the nineteenth century, British officialdom became increasingly worried that the volume of peasant indebtedness was growing and that its implications were becoming much more severe, as extending commercialisation gave land and its produce greater market value [66: 10–14]. These concerns fathered a broad historiography [65;71;75] which painted social change on the Indian land in dramatic hues: substantial land transfer and subinfeudation, as creditors, supported by the westernised legal system, attempted through foreclosing mortgages to secure peasant debtors' lands, and the subsequent creation of a new large agrarian proletariat. Besides the social impact, the economic consequences are clear. On this interpretation, the poorer peasantry faced intensifying poverty. At the same time, since the beneficiaries of change were often depicted as *nouveaux riches* moneylenders and traders with a parasitical attitude to agriculture, the land did not gain a new breed of 'improving' masters.

At first sight, this view of agrarian change has much to recommend it. It is supported by widespread contemporary comment. When, for example, Ravinder Kumar alleges substantial land transfer from peasant proprietors to alien moneylenders in the western India of the 1870s, he is merely reflecting the official explanation of the causes of the Deccan Riots, outbursts of agrarian protest in 1875 [75: *ch. 5*; 76: *ch. 1*]. The census material, too, does imply the creation of a large class of landless labourers over the last century of British rule [71]. And the dispossession and pauperisation of the poorer peasant proprietors would explain the paradox of frequent famine amidst the apparently most favourable period for agriculture in the second half of the nineteenth century.

Nevertheless, as with the impact of the land revenue systems, the trend of most modern scholarship has been to regard dramatic views of nineteenth-century agrarian change with scepticism. Again, the degree of turnover in landownership in the pre-British period is a relevant reservation; indeed, in Kessinger's Punjab village the great shift in control over the land occurred not in the British period but in the eighteenth century [68]. Most important, the social divisions evident by the twentieth century apparently always existed in some form; the modern landless labourers had their antecedents in traditional south Indian society [72] and tenancy was extensive in the eighteenth-century Maratha kingdom [58]. At the same time, the progressive trends of the late nineteenth century appear to have been exaggerated. Outsiders and *nouveaux riches* may have acquired significant landholdings at points of crisis, such as famine years, but this may have been merely temporary insurance by groups who had little long-term stake and interest in farming operations. Most modern regional and local studies in fact suggest a striking degree of continuity in overall patterns of landownership and control [66: *ch. 9*; 67;68;74]. And when more reliable statistics on occupation become available in the twentieth century, they do not suggest a markedly rising trend in the proportion of landless labourers within the rural population [73].

Of course, such relative stability in formal status may still mask considerable flux in economic relationships between groups. Even if creditors did not typically dispossess peasant debtors, forms of mortgage could be used as coercion, giving substantial powers over agricultural activities and production. Hower, the lenders who had such ambitions were, it seems, typically the more prosperous and thriving members of the peasant community rather than complete outsiders [52;53;54]. As a result, economic and social stratification within the peasantry has now emerged as a prominent theme in the literature on the late nineteenth century. Instead of the wily, *nouveau riche* moneylender thrusting his way into landownership, we now have the 'rich peasant', an established figure in the village, intensifying his wealth and power through more subtle measures of market control. The phrase covers a range of social groups; as well as cultivating landowners in the west and south [52;53;75], 'occupancy tenants' in the *taluqdari* regions, protected by legislation from 1859 [69: *ch. 5*], may have enjoyed sufficient independence from landlord control. For the key characteristic, it seems, is that the rich peasant enjoyed superior access to resources like credit, and greater ability to recognise and latch on to new commercial opportunities [52;53]. Stokes comments: 'there seems general agreement that the "golden age" of the rich peasant . . . spanned the period 1860–1900' [66: *275*], arguably the very era of most rapidly extending commercialisation.

Control by a rich peasantry lacks the socially revolutionary implications of the old assumptions about excessive land transfer, but its developmental lessons may be similar. Poor peasants may still have been pauperised whilst the rich became parasitic and highly conservative in their use of capital and income. Barrington Moore clearly has some such explanation in mind when he argues that 'Pax Britannica simply enabled the landlord . . . to pocket the economic surplus generated in the countryside that in Japan paid for the painful first stages of industrialisation' [70: *354–5*]. In similar vein, some, like Neale [63: *ch. 1*], stress the special attachment to and importance of land as a source of power and prestige within Indian society, arguably intensified during the nineteenth century amidst growing competition for and subdivision of ownership and revenue collection rights. The possibility remains, then, that agrarian social structure may have been peculiarly inhibitive of development.

To sustain the case, however, we would have to demonstrate that conditions in India were somehow different from other economies at equivalent stages of development. But were they? Similar credit and debt systems, for example, existed in most predominantly agrarian economies.[8] The commitment of substantial investment to land and local moneylending undoubtedly did and does pose fundamental problems for Indian development [57], but the apparently high rates of short-term return and the social and political *kudos* thus secured made these, rather than speculation in commercial or industrial ventures, the obvious outlets for those with capital. The real problem is one of comparable rates of return in other areas of the economy, a difficulty widely shared within less developed countries.

In general, recent research must cast considerable doubt on interpretations like Barrington Moore's. Orthodoxy now suggests that by 1900 a rich peasant cultivating élite existed in many regions. In turn, contrary to Moore, it is hard to see much distinction between this group and the Meiji landlord, so vaunted for his alleged contribution to Japanese development. Indeed, the Indian rich peasantry arguably enjoyed many of the same advantages – rising cash crop prices, control of local markets, even, perhaps, a declining real burden of land taxation by the late nineteenth century – which, it is claimed, enabled Japanese landlords to secure high rates of productive investment.

There remains substantial area for debate over economic and social relationships within the Indian countryside. The credit system, for example, can be seen as predominantly 'exploitative', maintaining and enhancing the power of established élites, or as functionalist, providing necessary short-term funds for an agricultural economy chronically lacking in capital. Again, there will continue to be controversy about the nature and extent of stratification, or how far, following McAlpin, the process was being crucially moderated by 1900. We might, however, venture the conclusion that, whatever the performance of agriculture, the rural social structure and its evolution over the nineteenth century in India was admirably attuned to the encouragement of capitalist development.

3 Business and Industrial Development

THE mid-nineteenth-century expectation was, as we earlier noted, of an imminent Indian industrial revolution, but, crucially, one based entirely on the rapid development of modern factory industry. Concerning India's traditional handicraft industries, the contemporary assumption – dramatised in Marx's famous phrase about 'the British intruder who broke up the Indian hand-loom and destroyed the spinning wheel' [5: 91] – was of grave decline created by competition from Western manufactured imports. Since, however, the actual development of the modern industrial sector proved sluggish and patchy, this latter interpretation has raised, for the subsequent historiography, fundamental issues about the overall progress of industrialisation in India. The problem can be presented most clearly in employment terms. As late as 1931, workers in modern factory industry totalled only just over 1·5 million out of a population of around 353 million [17: 136]. Obviously any substantial fall in activity in the handicrafts industry, more widely distributed within the economy, could have more than counterbalanced this, producing overall decline in industrial employment. At the outset of our investigation of industrialisation, then, we need to consider whether the effective trend in nineteenth-century India was actually towards 'de-industrialisation'.

Use of census data is one way of examining the thesis. In fact, the major censuses of the late British period do superficially suggest a significant decline in 'manufacturing employment' between 1881 and 1931, but the Thorners, in an early exercise of sophisticated statistical scepticism, demonstrated that this phenomenon was probably an artificial creation of changing enumeration techniques [20: ch. 6]. Their conclusion – that the distribution by occupation of the Indian workforce was probably not altering much – has since been supported by J. Krishnamurty for the first half of the twentieth century [80]. Whilst Krishnamurty's work suggests some shift towards agricultural employment in rural India, overall movements were 'at best marginal' and manufacturing's share of the workforce remained fairly constant at around 9 per cent between 1911 and 1951. For the bulk of the nineteenth century a statistical exercise like Krishnamurty's is impossible, but it now seems unlikely that substantial shifts in employment distribution were occurring, at any rate at all-India level. Nevertheless, the conclusions of the Thorners and Krishnamurty do delineate the scope of the problem. Even after 1880, when the growth of the modern sector accelerated, industry was no more than maintaining its share of the labour force. We can safely guess, then, that before 1880 the proportion was not growing; indeed, some slight process of 'de-industrialisation', in employment terms, may well then have been in train.

Can we, however, be more precise about the fate of handicraft industry? Clearly the textile export industry, which Raychaudhuri describes supplying South-east Asia, the Arab countries and East Africa in the eighteenth century [13: 85], collapsed (though there were some specialist exceptions like the shawl trade of Kashmir), but this was the usual fate of handicraft export in the nineteenth century and would have happened without formal British rule. For most handicraft producers – certainly outside Bengal – the home market must always have dominated and was, therefore, the crucial battleground. Here sales of British goods, particularly textiles, undoubtedly rose substantially during the nineteenth century. The value of British cotton goods exports, only just over £100,000 in 1813, rose to £5·2 million in 1850 and £18·4 million by 1896 [126: 91]. There is no doubt that this competition had a substantial impact on the Indian handicraft cotton industry and that the spinning sector probably experienced a serious setback during the early nineteenth century. However, some important reservations about the general extent of the process need consideration. Firstly, the volume of imports should be set in the context of the vast size of the Indian market. Kiernan comments that 'the sixty-four million yards of muslin imported into India in 1837 would not have given the population of British India one yard each', whilst the annual needs of a family of five might amount to eighty yards [25: 173]. In similar vein, Morris claims that imports may only have skimmed off the expansion of demand created by his rising per capita income [13: 9]. India, too, was not an easy market for British producers, since the smaller firms especially faced difficulties of founding and running efficient marketing organisations [128]. Again, imports were not always competing with home production. Typically they could not challenge local producers in tapping the lowest levels of demand in the village and some imports might even complement handicraft production. As late as 1900 £1·66 million worth out of nearly £20 million worth of imports of cotton manufactures were yarn imports and these, Morris argues [13: 9], may have helped some weavers by supplying them with a cheaper commodity. Furthermore, many traditional crafts, such as leather-making and tobacco-curing, experienced no serious threat, and some, like metal and woodworking, probably enjoyed significant growth.

Whilst, then, Indian cotton spinners were undoubtedly severely challenged, it is highly unlikely that any broad, permanent destruction of handicrafts in the face of competition from imports occurred. Indeed, the handicraft sector has undoubtedly remained important in the modern Indian economy. General statistics on the cotton industry, for example, suggest that only from about 1910 did factory production of piece-goods exceed that of the handlooms [82: 226–7]. However, advancing the discussion beyond such generalisation requires more specific studies than yet exist. Bagchi has recently pointed the way with an important short examination of the central Bihar region, suggesting a substantial decline in handicraft employment there; whilst estimates for 1809–13 record 18·6 per cent of the region's population as industrially employed, the equivalent figure available from the 1901 Census is only 8·5 per cent [78]. This seems a marked change, particularly since population had grown only slowly here. Even so, Bagchi's study reveals some of the difficulties of such work, notably problems of definition and of comparability of statistics, highlighted in Vicziany's sharp critique [79]. Since most handicraft work was part-time, combined with agricultural operations, it is hard to be precise about numbers 'industrially employed', especially for the early nineteenth century.

Nevertheless, Bagchi's study may indicate the general trend in the region, for it is likely that the Bengal Presidency, including Bihar, bore the brunt of any destructive impact of Western commercialism. The province came earliest under British rule, in the more blatantly exploitative age of the nabobs, and the intricate river systems of eastern India permitted effective penetration by European goods even in the pre-railway age. Elsewhere, however, – in, for example, western India – obstacles to commercial intrusion seem much more substantial. The Bombay Presidency was not acquired until 1818.

Further, the long mountain spur of the Western Ghats inhibited penetration into the interior until a network of local railways was complete, as late, in the case of many district towns, as the last years of the nineteenth century. Here, too, traditional handicraft industry was more geographically dispersed, less urban orientated and much more dependent on the home market than in Bengal, thus forming a less concentrated target for commercial competition. To stretch hypothesis even further, one might wonder whether this influenced the character of modern industrialisation in western and in eastern India. In the nineteenth century, Bengal factory industry, as we shall see, was overwhelmingly foreign owned and highly enclavist, whereas, in the Bombay Presidency, Indian ownership was more extensive and, by 1900, there was already some diversification of the cotton industry into district centres like Ahmedabad and Sholapur. A more flourishing recent performance in handicrafts in western India may possibly have provided some industrial traditions, linkages and opportunities for this.

This, however, is guesswork. At the present state of knowledge, we can suggest that the thesis of marked 'de-industrialisation' has not yet been sustained. The most sensible conclusion would be that the overall performance of the handicraft sector was fairly neutral in impact on the nineteenth-century economy, though this is an aggregate impact composed of many variations between different crafts and regions.

Even this, however, may tell us something about the problems of Indian industrialisation. One might argue that if extensive industrial development was to occur in an economy like nineteenth-century India's, then a substantial and complementary process of expansion in both handicraft and modern industrial sectors was required. This pattern of dualistic development may, strikingly, have occurred in Meiji Japan where much industrialisation was of the small-scale, handicraft type, and where, additionally, the modern and traditional sectors were often linked in interdependence by sub-contracting arrangements. In nineteenth-century India, in contrast, it seems unlikely that handicraft industry was, in general, a significant source of growth. This, in turn, may have influenced the apparent reluctance of rural capital to look beyond investment in land and moneylending. In sum, for India, a neutral performance by the vital traditional industrial sector may have been by no means good enough.

The de-industrialisation thesis implies, as well as decline in the handicrafts, a limited view of the performance of modern business and industry; but any investigation of this area has to begin by acknowledging the growth of a substantial modern industrial sector in the period after 1850. The steady expansion of the pioneer industries, cotton and jute textiles, was such that by 1914 India stood as the world's fourth greatest cotton manufacturing nation [15: 262]. Progress, too, in the provision of modern communications was considerable. By 1913 India boasted nearly 34,000 miles of railway, just over half the total for Asia (including the Russian Asiatic territories and the Middle East) and more than each of the continents of Africa and Australasia [123: 22]. Any reader tempted to a simple view of Indian 'industrial backwardness' might reflect that capacity in the Indian cotton spinning industry still exceeded that in the Japanese equivalent by nearly three times in 1914 [84: 335,367], a date when some would characterise Japan as having already achieved a cotton-led industrial take-off.

Modern industrial development was dominated by the consumer industries. As late as 1930 around 45 per cent of all factory employees worked in the cotton and jute mills [17: 136], and the textile industries, with food and tobacco added, unquestionably provided more than half manufacturing's contribution to GNP throughout the British period. This leads Kidron to speak of 'unbalanced growth' [111: 21], but most non-Western follower industrialisers – contemporary Japan and Brazil, even Russia during the first half of the nineteenth century – initially experienced most rapid development in the consumer sectors and encountered marked technical backwardness or 'lateness' in heavy industry. In fact British India's heavy industrial development was not as rudimentary as is sometimes assumed. Coal production, mainly based on the Raniganj and Jharia fields in the Bengal Presidency, began to expand rapidly in the late nineteenth and early twentieth centuries as demand from the railways was increasingly channelled towards Indian coal. By 1914 total production exceeded fifteen million tons per annum and India had become a net exporter of coal [85]. Exploitation of the Jharia coalfield, with its coking coal resources, also offered the first opportunities for large-scale modern iron and steel production. The great plant at Jamshedpur, 150 miles west of Calcutta, was constructed by the cotton magnate, J. N. Tata, from 1907, and, after initial problems, production expanded swiftly in response to the shortages of the First World War and tariff protection thereafter [82: *ch. 9*]. Even here performance did not much lag behind Japan, where construction of the Yawata works, the first modern iron and steel plant, only began in the late 1890s.

Nor were the leading Indian plants technically unsophisticated. Buchanan, writing in 1934, could describe Jamshedpur as 'one of the largest and best equipped iron and steel plants in the world' [17: *285*]. The Tata Iron and Steel Company, too, by direct acquisition of coal mines during the 1910s, had created a strong, vertically integrated business unit much like the Ruhr concerns [88]. In the cotton industry, Tatas installed ring spinning at their Empress Mills at Nagpur in the early 1880s, whilst Lancashire was still reliant on mule spinning [14: *139*]. As the cotton industry expanded over the late nineteenth century, it developed increasing exports of yarn to other Asian countries, particularly China. From the transition to net export of yarn during the early 1880s, by 1914 India stood second only to Britain as a world exporter of cotton yarns [121: *189*].

Nevertheless, the limitations of modern industrialisation in the nineteenth century also need great emphasis. India entirely lacked the major 'new' industries, such as chemicals and heavy electricals, which in Europe seemed vital to successful rapid industrial development after 1870. Modern industry, too, remained a very thinly spread phenomenon; the industrial census of 1911 recorded only just over 7000 units throughout British India employing more than twenty workers and more than a third of these did not use mechanical power [16: *121*]. Growth rates, it appears, were slow, and industrial development was beset by short-term fluctuations. The whole decade from 1896 to 1905, for example, saw 'a very severe trade depression' in the cotton industry [16: *104–5*]. Most strikingly, regional enclavism was pronounced. In 1900 over half the capacity in the cotton industry was situated in Bombay City [82: *234*]. Thereafter new centres did develop but still mainly in western India and as late as 1931 nearly two-thirds of all cotton mills were located in the Bombay Presidency, overwhelmingly in Bombay City, Ahmedabad or Sholapur [17: *201*]. In contrast, the jute, coal and iron and steel industries were substantially Bengal phenomena, and even here there was a sharp divide between Calcutta, commercial metropolis and centre of the jute industry, and the heavy industrial belt to the west. Modern industrialisation in the India of 1900 was, therefore, fundamentally concentrated in three isolated enclaves –

Bombay City, Calcutta and the west Bengal/Bihar coal belt – with strictly limited impact on one another and on other regions.

These characteristics might be explained in terms of the poverty of the grass-roots economy and problems of raw material supply and location. Clearly the rate of growth of demand for industrial goods was likely to be slow and variable. The onset of depression in the Bombay cotton industry during the late 1890s might seem unsurprising when potential customers were faced with famine. Industry, too, understandably developed close to sources and channels of supply: Bombay the focus of trade routes from diverse cotton growing regions like Berar, Gujarat and Dharwar, and Calcutta the natural recipient of the Bengal countryside's jute. For heavy industry, India did not lack absolutely resources of both coal and iron ore, but most Indian coal was bituminous. Good quality coking coal for iron and steel manufacture was largely confined to the west Bengal belt and, in particular, to the Jharia field.

Nevertheless, even within the parameters imposed by supply and demand conditions, modern industrialisation still seemed a sluggish process. The home market for the textile industries, for example, even if poor was potentially vast, but Indian industry had great difficulty in capturing it. Imports of cotton piece-goods, mainly of course from Britain, were still rising substantially in the early twentieth century, and in 1910–11 stood at double the total production of piece-goods by Indian mills [82: 226]. Whilst, as we shall see later, imperial policy – notably the absence of significant tariff protection – might be assigned root blame, the simple cause of this lay in the nature of Indian production. The nineteenth-century Indian cotton industry was overwhelmingly a spinning industry, producing yarns much more than finished cloth. Of all the cotton mills in existence in 1903–4, just over half were entirely devoted to spinning but only six exclusively to weaving [84: 367].

Such imbalances were not unknown in early follower industrialisation; the Russian modern cotton industry, for example, as it emerged in the 1820s and 1830s, was fundamentally a weaving industry, using imported yarn. In India's case, perhaps, the imbalance might be justified, in developmental terms, because of the increasing value of yarn exports during the late nineteenth century. This expansion, however, proved of limited long-term impact. Within a few years, the whirlwind of Japanese export expansion devastated some of Indian yarn's most prominent markets. In 1906 India supplied over three-quarters of all yarn imports into China but by

1914 Japan had become the largest single supplier, and ten years later India met under a quarter of the Chinese yarn market [84: *148*].

This crushing defeat in a vital export battleground says more about the competitiveness of Indian compared with Japanese industry than any number of painstaking economic calculations. And its consequences were considerable. Whilst, with the aid of protection, in the inter-war period the Indian cotton industry developed a much stronger weaving and finishing dimension and captured much of the home market, it proved largely incapable of breaking into world markets for finished cloth. During the 1930s the cotton industry was to supply under 2 per cent, by value, of India's total exports. Jute products, it is true, significantly improved their performance, raising their share of exports from 2·6 per cent in 1890–1 to 14·5 per cent by 1935–6. Yet they faced substantial international competition and demand varied considerably according to fluctuations in levels of world trade.

Hence, even in the leading sectors, industry was struggling to meet home demand whilst failing to establish itself on any permanent scale in world export markets. Despite the marked decline in imports under tariff protection after 1914, India remained in 1939 a net importer of cotton goods. In the crucial contrast with Japan, this was a striking difference. Japan was able to escape from limitations of demand imposed by a poor and slowly expanding home market: India was not.

How can we explain this? Perhaps the most familiar answers are in terms of India's imperial subjection: problems associated with foreign ownership of business and industry, India's role in the British Empire and alleged shortcomings of government policy. The debates on these questions are detailed and will require separate consideration. First, however, we need to consider another fundamental issue, that of the indigenous response to business and industrial opportunity.

(iii) THE SOCIAL RESPONSE TO MODERNISATION

Max Weber's belief that in India capitalism necessarily had to be 'taken over as a finished artifact without autonomous beginnings' [99: *4*] raised the concept that religious and cultural beliefs and practices had inhibited the spontaneous emergence of modern business activity. India, however, never lacked trading communities and sophisticated commercial organisation [91]. Indeed, recent studies of the 'traditional' merchant present a striking impression of diversity of function and initiative; even among Marwari family firms, Timberg distinguishes three clear types, 'the "great" multi-branch trading firms, the banians and brokers in the major export and import markets, and the speculators in futures' [95: 3]. Further, merchant communities in 1800 were not timid, servile dependents of a hostile system. Both Gillion on Ahmedabad [92] and Bayly on Benares [93] describe something of a 'burgher ethic' in the cities and the latter characterises his Benares merchants as 'a high status commercial community whose economic organisations and "moral community" breached caste and neighbourhood boundaries in many important aspects' [93: 172].

Such groups, clearly, should have been capable of playing a dynamic role in an expanding industrial economy. However, in the nineteenth century, indigenous merchant activity, with the conspicuous exception of that in Bombay City, was relatively little converted into industrial enterprise. Indian capital remained largely engaged, in Ray's phrase, in 'comprador activities' [83: 4], peripheral mercantile pursuits. Timberg's great Marwari firms, for example – among the wealthiest of all Indian commercial interests – seemed highly hesitant about breaking into industry. Only in 1918–19 did G. D. Birla and Sarupchand Hukumchand set up the first large Indian controlled jute mills, and then from the security of massive speculation profits acquired during the First World War inflation [95: 34].

Why was this? Any social value orientated interpretation faces difficulty, if only because of the often eager response to opportunity within the 'comprador activities'. The American Civil War boom, for example, in providing a substantial boost to the cotton trade, provoked massive speculation in Bombay. Many new banks and financial companies were founded, predominantly to handle cotton marketing, and Rungta estimates that the paid-up capital of new companies registered in India between 1863 and 1865 totalled as much as Rs 206 million [86: 257]. This may suggest that the problem, so far from any absence of commercial initiative, was excessive response to the most attractive short-term opportunities at the expense of other areas of the developing economy. The cotton trade, in particular, proliferated middlemen; in the Bombay business there was 'a battery of intermediaries' [96: 177], including commodity dealers, marketers, handlers, brokers and *shroffs*. Such numbers dealing and speculating in export trades may, also, have induced greater instability in the economy as a whole. The 'boom and bust' cycle of 1863–5 in Bombay provides an obvious example, but over half a century later the inflation of the First World War era was greatly exacerbated by speculation in cash crops, inducing the Bombay government to try to control by legislation the city's raw cotton trade [97: 200].

On this interpretation, then, the very sophistication of traditional Indian business organisation provoked a type of commercial involution, when dramatic new stimuli were presented to it in the nineteenth century. As the Industrial Commission Report of 1919 noted, indigenous capital, as was 'rational', rushed to short-term, speculative trading opportunities, preventing its widespread utilisation in the industrial sector. The problem, however, can be viewed in a more basic way. The history of Birla and Sarupchand Hukumchand's move into the jute industry might simply suggest the scale of capital resources required to invest in modern factory industry. Indian 'merchant capital', one might argue, was in general too weak to promote large-scale industrialisation. The Tatas, for example, faced crippling financial costs in the early development of Jamshedpur; the extension programme inaugurated in 1916 even necessitated guarantees of a permanent share of profits to their leading creditor [83: 27]. At root, too, is the problem of comparative rates of return. Just as in the rural economy capital was attracted to land and moneylending, so too in the business economy dealing in cotton may have offered greater security, and certainly opportunity for larger windfall gains, than any industrial investment.

The problem, nevertheless, is complicated, because in the cotton industry, as we shall see, Indian entrepreneurship was much more extensive than elsewhere in the modern sector. Even so, such complexities would hardly suggest that general values and beliefs, in the Weberian tradition, were a significant influence [100]. More convincing is Morris's recent emphasis on differential knowledge of markets and opportunities [102], since this can explain variations: arguably the cotton industry's mass consumer markets were much more familiar and 'knowable' to indigenous entrepreneurs than jute's commercial and international markets.

The social response to industrialisation, however, has been most fully studied in the modern literature from the industrial labour front. Here, again, no especially 'Asiatic' problems emerge, for the clear conclusion is that 'the supply of labour responded positively to the growing demand from the expanding factory' [107: 325]. There

41

seems to have been no serious absolute shortage of labour for modern industry. Indeed, the existence, in the Bombay cotton industry, of large numbers of surplus *badlis*, temporary workers employed on a day-to-day basis, 'suggests that the state of excess supply of labour was a normal one' [104: *478*]. Labour came to the great centres of Bombay and Calcutta from as far afield as the Delhi region [103;106;107] and problems of industrial relations and discipline seem no greater than in other follower industrialisers at equivalent stages. Nomadism – periodic return by workers to their home villages, often to assist in agricultural operations – was undoubtedly extensive in the nineteenth century, but by 1900 a more permanent and urban orientated labour force was clearly evident in both Bombay and Calcutta [103;106].

It remains possible that patterns of labour organisation were inefficient and wasteful. Workers in many industries, notably cotton, were recruited by jobbers, who also controlled the *badlis* and acted as industrial foremen. This extensive power created opportunities for corruption: jobbers had, for example, an apparent vested interest in rapid labour turnover and absenteeism, because they could obtain commissions from new workers and *badlis* they engaged. Such a system, however, was not unique to India, for in Japan, too, labour for the cotton mills was engaged and controlled by intermediaries, the 'recruiting agents'. In both countries employers acquiesced in these arrangements and it may even be, as Newman suggests [105], that the Indian jobber system at root provided an effective social device for assimilating the workforce to factory employment. Only one major distinction, arguably, differentiated the Indian industrial labour force of 1900 from that in Japan. In India the workforce was largely male – over 80 per cent of the workers in the Bombay cotton industry in 1931 were men [17: *212*] – whereas in Japanese consumer industries female labour predominated. Early factory industrialisation, then, in Japan, as in Britain, may have especially benefited from drawing on a cheap labour reserve, which at the same time did not poach heavily on the male workforce in agriculture. Nevertheless, many economies industrialised sharing the Indian characteristic where few women were initially attracted to factory employment.

The labour market, in sum, may have had its limitations and inefficiencies, but it seems hard to regard it as a major obstacle to industrial growth in the nineteenth century. Whilst serious work remains necessary on labour cost and on availability of skilled labour, on simple supply we can safely conclude with Morris that 'it was not difficult to create an industrial labour force in India' [103: *208*].

Nineteenth-century India, then, seems characterised by a generally flexible social response to modernisation. Traditional bogeys like caste appear to have had less impact than often assumed: Bayly on merchant organisation [93] and Newman and Misra on industrial labour [105;106], for example, all play down caste's role as a dominant social organisation. However, the problems we have outlined in this chapter – the probable lack of dynamism in the handicraft sector, the sluggish progress of modern industrialisation, the faltering translation of indigenous merchant enterprise into industrial activity – still require explanation. We must next examine the conditions directly created by the imperial connection.

4 Investment, Trade and the Imperial Connection

BRITISH rule inextricably connected India with the international financial and commercial economy, unleashing during the nineteenth century a range of new influences and forces upon the sub-continent's development. Of these, one of the most striking was a large inflow of foreign capital. Whilst statistics, especially on the period before 1870, cannot be definitive, it seems that the total volume of British investment in India stood at about £160 million in 1870 rising to £380 million by 1913 [125: *341*]. The 1870 figure perhaps then represented some 20 per cent of all British overseas investment but thereafter the tendency was for investment in India to rise less rapidly than elsewhere so that the proportion by 1913 was probably around 10 per cent. Even so, these amounts must still have been substantial within the context of an economy chronically short of capital and by 1914 possibly up to three-quarters of total investment in modern business and industry in India had come from abroad [123: *55*]. One obvious consequence was extensive foreign ownership within the modern sector. Again, precise statistical assessment is difficult, but by Independence, certainly, the foreign share of capital invested was around or above three-quarters in key areas such as jute, mining, tea planting and shipping [111: *4*].

The effects of this on the Indian economy are a matter of intense debate. Raychaudhuri argues that foreign investment distorted industrial development by producing 'merely ... the growth of enclaves, their linkage effects being confined to a minimum' [13: *96*]. This charge is based on foreign capital's propensity, evident in many less-developed countries, to concentrate on transport, extractive or export industries. In India, in fact, the main thrust came overwhelmingly in railways: between 1845 and 1875 alone an estimated amount of nearly £100 million was sunk into guaranteed railway loans [115: *177*]. In sum, over a third of British investment in the sub-continent down to 1910 apparently went directly into railways. This, though, considerably underestimates their importance, for government loans took the largest slice of the foreign capital inflow – just under a half in 1910 – and their constructive use was dominated by railway building.

This preference for the public utilities, when linked with the general importance of foreign capital, gave a curious shape to the overall pattern of investment. Private manufacturing industry inevitably lagged, in comparison, as a recipient and at the outbreak of the First World War the paid-up share capital of all joint-stock companies amounted only to an estimated 17.9 per cent of total investments [17: *154*]. Put crudely, all private modern business and industry seems to have received less than a third of the capital invested in the railways during the nineteenth century. Within manufacturing industry foreign investment was still, of course, very important, but, even here, its distribution included marked variations. In one major industry, cotton, foreign investment and ownership was conspicuous by its relative absence: of 129 textile mills (overwhelmingly cotton mills) in the Bombay Presidency in 1911, only twelve were owned by companies with exclusively non-Indian directors and ninety-two were entirely Indian owned [82: *183*]. This contrasted dramatically with the situation in the other major textile industry, jute, where there was a monopoly of foreign ownership of modern mills in 1911. This reflected a notable regional distinction between the Bengal and Bombay Presidencies. In Bengal, besides European dominance over jute, mining and plantations, foreign ownership bit deep into the local economy, including activities such as printing. In western India – although the Europeans even here may have been tightening their control over sectors like the export trade during the late nineteenth century [96] – Indian business activity was undoubtedly more extensive, controlling not only the cotton mills but also modern food production through ownership of flour and rice mills.

The structure of foreign investment was, then, as Raychaudhuri charges, sharply enclavist, exercising at every level distinctive preferences. Undoubtedly Indian industrialisation might have been more expeditiously promoted if foreign capital had been distributed more broadly within manufacturing industry. However, this does not automatically mean that Indian development would have been smoother without foreign investment; indeed, one might argue that the foreign capital inflow was not extensive enough, for, viewed more closely, its historical pattern, as well as its distribution, was uneven. Before the 1840s much British investment in mercantile activities, in Jenks's words, 'represented simply portions of the Indian spoil and revenue reinvested in India' [110: *208*]. Thereafter, there were undoubtedly large new capital flows to finance railway construction [115], but before 1900 the attractiveness of India as a field for investment was diminishing. Increasingly, 'foreign investment' in India apparently represented the reinvestment of profits rather than an infusion of entirely new funds, and the nemesis of the 1930s saw a substantial repatriation of British investment [83: *14*]. Again, relative to the vast size of the Indian economy, volumes were always low. Maddison estimates that by 1938 India had received a smaller amount of foreign capital investment per head than any other equivalent economy except China [19: *55*]. And as we shall see, any outflows to foreign investors, throughout the peak period for investment in the half century before 1914, were never sufficient to endanger the balance of payments surplus which India then enjoyed. Saul comments that greater and more evenly distributed British investment in India was probably not a realistic prospect: to have brought per capita investment to the level of the major Dominions, he claims, would have required quadrupling total British overseas investment [121: *206*]. This, however, perhaps reveals the scale of the Indian problem. The wealthiest economy in the nineteenth-century world – exporting capital, some would say, at a rate which endangered supply to her own industry – sank a reasonable proportion of her foreign investment in India, only to create limited, enclavist development.

Nevertheless, even on the assumption that India desperately required capital of any type, foreign investment and ownership may have set up barriers as well as stimulants to development, particularly if it distorted the institutional structure of the economy. Its most insidious impact may have been to slow the emergence of indigenous infrastructural arrangements in support of business and industry; the foreigner with his independent contacts and sources of capital did not need them. Although modern companies began to emerge in India during the 1820s and 1830s in the wake of the break-up of the old Agency Houses, they encountered serious organisational problems. The absence of legal recognition of limited liability before legislation in the 1850s and 1860s merely, of course, mirrored Britain's own situation, but was perhaps a more serious deficiency in a large, backward economy. More important, there were no formal Indian stock exchanges. Dealers in shares and securities in Calcutta met under a tree and in Bombay in a crowded city street where, apparently, they faced the possibility of being moved on by the police for causing an obstruction. Only the construction of the Stock Exchange Building in 1899 finally removed the danger of this indignity, whilst in Calcutta the Stock Exchange was not formally constituted until 1908 [86: ch. 11].

Such deficiencies, again, might well have existed in the absence of extensive foreign investment, yet foreign ownership also appeared to create particular institutional peculiarities. Perhaps the most striking of these was the managing agency system, involving, as Kling defines it, 'the vesting of the management of a joint stock company in the hands of a firm of professional managers' [87: 37n]. The managing agency evolved out of the burgeoning activities of the early nineteenth-century Agency House and accompanying desire by British capital for careful supervision of its Indian investments. From around the 1860s, however, use of such a controlling organisation steadily became widespread throughout large-scale business and industry, even within Indian-owned companies. As late as 1955 the concerns controlled by managing agencies accounted for nearly three-quarters of the total paid-up capital invested in public companies [87:38].

The case for the managing agency – like that for the Japanese *zaibatsu* and the German joint stock bank – is that it could promote innovation, cost cutting and business efficiency. In particular, during the initial development of modern business and industry in the early and mid-nineteenth century, managing agencies were arguably valuable sources of managerial and technical talent and important channels for mobilising capital. Socially however – again the accusation levelled against German banks and Japanese *zaibatsu* – the system involved intense concentration of control. Even shareholders of companies were often excluded from any real knowledge or influence. Buchanan tells how during the late 1920s one agency would hold the half-yearly company meetings of five large jute mills in successive periods of five minutes each [17: 169]. In India this concentration of power also had racial implications. The large European-owned managing agency tended to employ European staff and to look to European expertise and capital, inhibiting the training of Indians in management and technical skills.

Further, the control exercised by the managing agency was such that an inefficient or even corrupt agency could inevitably destroy

47

dependent viable concerns. In 1878 the failure of Kessowji, Naik and Company – involving charges of criminal mismanagement against the directors – led to companies owning four cotton mills going into liquidation [86: *234*]. In general, it seems likely that the managing agency system became less advantageous and more costly over time. For the first half of the nineteenth century – perhaps down to 1870 – when capital and business expertise especially required mobilisation, it may have performed a necessary and viable function. Yet the managing agency was born of the early nineteenth-century system of commerce and exchange and its competence in handling the modern high technology industry which was starting to emerge by 1914 is more questionable: the Tata Iron and Steel Company, as Simmons reveals, were to face constant problems with the managing agencies they employed [88].

However, one might again comment of the managing agency, as of foreign capital and ownership in general, that it is hard to see how India could have been positively better off without it. The problem should be stated in a different way: arguably in nineteenth-century India the positive impetus of the foreign business stimulus was circumscribed by the pronounced dualism which its nature and the institutional forms it developed created. This dualism was exemplified in banking. A thriving modern banking sector, promoted by European interests, emerged in the great Presidency cities, but it enjoyed minimal links with the vast indigenous credit system. Even the wealthiest *shroffs* had little dealings with the Westernised banks [138:*9*]. Again, modern stock exchanges were slow to develop precisely because the managing agencies, with their own access to capital sources, by-passed them. This type of dualism itself set up further obstacles to the thoroughgoing modernisation of the Indian economy. By developing in enclaves, foreign activity implicitly struck a deal with traditional business whereby the latter, left free to pursue the wider opportunities of the nineteenth century in fields little touched by the foreigner, was strengthened rather than weakened.

(ii) THE FOREIGN TRADE SECTOR

Another major element in India's incorporation into the nineteenth-century international economy was the transformation of the country's foreign trade position. Firstly, the sheer volume of transactions grew at a rapid rate: between 1870 and 1914 alone the value of exports increased nearly five times [124: *35*]. Such dynamism had a deep-seated impact on Indian society. It helped to accomplish a substantial shift in power and influence away from the Ganges Plain, the traditional heartland of India, to the maritime provinces and in particular to the three great ports of Calcutta, Bombay and Madras. However, the character of India's foreign trade also changed. Chaudhuri points to the developing process in the period 1828–40 when the estimated value of cotton piece-goods exported from India fell by 48 per cent, whilst cotton yarn imports, by value, increased by 80 per cent and imports of cotton goods by 55 per cent [119: *347*]. Fundamentally India, as has already been implicit, became an exporter of agricultural produce and an importer of manufactured goods and equipment.

Nevertheless, this characteristic did not necessarily prevent the foreign trade sector from playing a constructive developmental role within the economy. Down to 1870 demand for Indian crops and their value in export markets was growing, spectacularly in the case of cotton during the American Civil War boom of the early 1860s [45]. Thereafter, the threat posed by the 'Great Depression' of 1873–96, when agricultural prices slumped on world markets, was tempered by monetary developments within the Indian economy. Silver, since 1835 the only legal tender in India, experienced marked depreciation for the mid 1870s as a result of large increases in world production and consequently the value of the silver rupee fell by about a third between 1874 and 1892 [148;149]. Devaluation created costs, particularly, as we shall see, in meeting international debts and charges paid in gold, but it also achieved what Rothermund calls the 'miracle' of stable export prices over the late nineteenth century [148: *99*], hence firmly stimulating Indian foreign trade. Rothermund's judgement – that this 'export bonus . . . imposed a pattern of trade on India which was not to its advantage' [148: *99*] – is not necessarily substantiated by events elsewhere. Japan, predominantly an exporter of raw silk and tea in the Meiji period, enjoyed the same 'export bonus' from a depreciating currency and for her, as for the British Dominions, export of agricultural produce during the nineteenth century proved stimulant rather than impediment to long-term development.

Of course, for Japan and others eventual export diversification was vital, but as Chaudhuri comments [117: *32*], the Indian situation was not static during the nineteenth century. Exports of jute and cotton manufactures expanded to provide over 14 per cent of total exports by 1910 [124: *37*], helping to counterbalance the substantial decline after 1870 in opium exports to China. The destination of exports also widened. Britain was the dominant outlet for much of the nineteenth century, receiving over half India's exports in 1870; but thereafter the proportion declined steadily, as India's trade with Europe and America became increasingly important. By 1910 Britain took just a quarter of India's exports, less than Europe and Asia individually [124:*37*].

Nevertheless, Indian imports, it is often assumed, remained substantially, even increasingly, determined by the imperial connection. The familiar charge is that from 1870 British industry, faced with growing competition and tariff walls in established Western markets, turned to the 'soft markets' of the Empire, particularly India, to find her customers. India's advance from Britain's third largest single customer in 1870 to the most important in 1913 appears to support this, for the proportion of total Britsh exports received by India had doubled over this period [125: *339*]. However, India's trade was now growing, in quantitative terms, at a faster rate than Britain's, so that the British share of total Indian imports was declining slowly from 84 per cent in 1870 to 62 per cent by 1910 [124: *40*]. A more serious issue, arguably, than the country of origin was the nature of imports. Nineteenth-century Indian imports were strongly orientated towards consumer goods and, for a follower industrialiser, technology and equipment featured relatively lowly. The problem, then, was not necessarily the dominance of the metropolitan power as a supplier but the traditional importance of particular British exporters – notably the Lancashire cotton industry – within Indian markets, to the relative neglect even of other British industrial interests. Imports were still not without some productive impact, for Lancashire's archetypal export to India was unfinished 'grey goods', which required, at the least, dyeing and printing in India [126: *101*]. However, the character of imports undoubtedly suggested the squandering of developmental opportunities, particularly in weak sectors like capital goods, electricals and chemicals, which might have been stimulated by greater imports of technology.

Not only does the nature of imports raise questions, but also their overall scale. Throughout the nineteenth century India typically enjoyed a substantial surplus on her merchandise balance of trade. In fact, after 1830 the only deficit occurred during the period 1855–63. Sometimes, too, the surplus was of massive proportions: during the middle years of the 1860s, for example, it exceeded total imports in value [124: *35*]. This surplus was earned through favourable balances with most trading partners: Europe, America and in particular Asia.

This is one of the most important features of India's economic position in the nineteenth century, involving fundamental issues. Clearly it initially suggests a capacity of exports consistently to exceed demand for imported goods, but on closer examination its very occurrence is a puzzle. A poor country, presumably desperate for imports of capital goods, should have been able to liquidate any trade surplus to great advantage. To examine the problem fully, we need to widen the debate.

(iii) THE IMPERIAL CONNECTION

The simple answer traditionally offered is that the surplus was a consequence of imperial subjection: that British economic needs required and insisted upon its maintenance. Indeed, India's whole foreign trade position is frequently presented as fundamental to the British-centred world economy of the nineteenth century, especially in the years before the First World War, when India allegedly formed 'the pivot of the international settlement system' [122: *35*]. The key to this is that India, despite the overall surplus, was increasingly in trading deficit with Britain from the 1870s, at the very time when British commercial hegemony faced serious challenge [121]. From the British point of view this relationship, since India enjoyed substantial surpluses with her other trading partners, proved highly convenient, counterbalancing her own growing deficits with Europe and North America; hence the familiar comment that India was 'financing' more than two-fifths of British trading deficits by the outbreak of the First World War [121: *62*; 125: *340*].

Some such interconnection of British and Indian trade was not new. During the early nineteenth century Indian exports of opium to China played a vital role in paying for Britain's large purchases of China tea. Undoubtedly Britain benefited from these relationships, but their effect on India and the precise degree of colonial manipulation and control involved are more complex issues. British-centred accounts of the international economy may create a false impression of an ordered, schematised and historically stable system. Yet the international pattern of multilateral payments, in which India features so prominently, operated in so organised a way only briefly in the two or three decades before 1914. Again, the triangular trade involving Indian opium and China tea was always unstable in view of the Chinese authorities' hostility to opium imports. India's foreign trade position was constantly evolving. Hence, although the imperial rulers influenced the situation through general attempts to promote exports and, specifically, through government purchasing policy (which we shall examine in the next chapter), British benefit from India's foreign trade structure was perhaps the outcome of historical conjuncture. Strikingly, the existence of India's large foreign trade surplus antedated the emergence of the particular conditions whereby India seemed to be 'financing' British deficits in the late nineteenth century. Throughout the middle third of the nineteenth century, in fact, India normally enjoyed a comfortable surplus on merchandise trade with Britain. The deficit which thereafter developed remained small down to 1880.

Nevertheless, India's general trading surplus may have been necessitated by quite specific conditions created by imperial rule: namely the famous 'drain'. If profits paid to foreign investors, charges for freight and banking and in particular the 'home charges', in Dutt's phrase, drained 'the life-blood of India in a continuous, ceaseless flow' [2: xiv], then clearly meeting the burden would continually demand a substantial surplus on merchandise trade.

The existence of some 'drain' can hardly be disputed. It was self-evident down to 1833 when the government of British territories was also a private company continuing to trade (in fact before 1813 the official monopolist of the Indian trade). During this period the East India Company was prepared to use the Indian public revenues not just to settle overseas debt and administrative charges but also to meet financial obligations to its own shareholders. Remembering the drive to maximise land revenue receipts in this era, resources, it might be argued, were being directly expropriated to Britain from the Indian land, and the 'remittance problem' became widely noted in early nineteenth-century writings [118]. Then, during the 1830s, the issue acquired a different dimension as Indian governments started to borrow heavily in Britain, in particular to finance the expensive, expansionary wars of the period: the taxpayer in British India now seemed to be acquiring new burdens to ensure the subjection of other Indians. Servicing the public debt, though, was merely one of the 'home charges' which preoccupied critics during the second half of the nineteenth century. As Sir George Wingate remarked in 1859, India was charged for her administration on a totally different basis from the white colonies [2: *xvi*]. The Indian taxpayer met all administrative expenses incurred within Britain as well as in India, paying, for example, the wages of the charladies who cleaned the corridors of the India Office in London. All such charges, of course, became more burdensome during the progressive devaluation of the silver rupee in the late nineteenth century.

How great was the drain? Dutt's assessment was that 'one-fourth of all the revenues derived in India is annually remitted to England', amounting to £159 million out of total revenues of £647 million over the last decade of Victoria's reign [2: *xiv*]. Such contemporary estimates, however, can be challenged on their definition of what constituted the drain. Often costs were included, notably profits paid to foreign investors, which were borne by many developing economies in the nineteenth century, outside normal definitions of Britain's 'informal' let alone formal empire. Most modern measurement, therefore, has concentrated on the home charges: interest paid to Britain on the Indian public debt, military charges (notably the cost of maintaining the Indian Army), the cost of purchasing 'stores' in Britain and the 'civil charges' arising from British administration, the latter including those India Office charladies and, especially, payment of Civil Service salaries and pensions. Even many of these charges, however, might not be viewed, strictly, as a 'drain'. The rapid growth of the Indian public debt, for example – it stood at £30 million in 1837 and £220 million by 1900 [129: *203*] – was mirrored in other contemporary developing economies, such as Russia, where foreign borrowing is frequently ascribed a highly productive role. In fact much of India's public debt, like Russia's, was the outcome of expenditure on railway building, which presumably had some constructive impact. The drain, then, is now typically defined as the unproductive element in the 'home charges'. In this light Macpherson points to 'defence services', which totalled around 15 per cent of the home charges in 1870, along with civil pensions and allowances [14: *156*]. Similarly, T. Mukerjee estimates that between 1840 and 1900 some 18 per cent of the public debt was caused by wars [129: *204*].

Pared down in this way, the drain looks much less like Dutt's 'continuous, ceaseless flow'. Mukerjee assesses it, defined as 'unnecessary' home charges, at about £42 million over the 1840–1900 period [129: *205*]. By any standards this must have been an infinitesimal percentage of total national income: Mukerjee suggests between 0.04 and 0.07 over the period 1870–1900 [129: *205*]. Even if all the home charges are included, the drain would barely exceed 0.5 per cent of national income.

Undoubtedly this modern measurement correctly highlights, in simple quantitative terms, what Chaudhuri calls the 'insignificance' of the drain controversy [117: 43]. It is perhaps remarkable that so much attention has been expended on the late nineteenth-century expropriatory mechanism whilst the massive new mobilisation of revenue funds associated with early British rule remains comparatively ignored.[9] However, the more sophisticated drain theorists were also identifying a general imbalance in India's external relationships: Naoroji, indeed, regarded railway construction with borrowed capital as a 'mitigating factor' [130: 23]. In fact, the quantitative insignificance of the drain merely emphasises that imbalance, for clearly, if the real drain was very small, it by no means offsets and explains the foreign trade surplus. The difference, of course, may represent large profits expropriated by foreign investors in private companies, but, despite the absence of definitive modern work in this area, it seems clear that profits were often reinvested rather than permanently repatriated to Britain. In any case, we know that the drain, even in its widest, nineteenth-century definition, could not have counterbalanced the surplus on merchandise trade, for the simple reason that India was a net importer of treasure. This treasure inflow, as Latham remarks, 'can be taken to represent the net benefit to India from her external transactions' [124: 36].

How great, then, was the treasure inflow and what was its significance? Undoubtedly it was large in quantitative terms: one assessment is that the net inflow of silver into India between 1861 and 1895 totalled one third of world silver output during the period [149: 64]. Theoretically such treasure imports should have had a marked stimulatory effect by considerably expanding the money supply, but one recent investigation suggests 'little or no correlation between the net influx of silver and changes in the money measure' [149: 63]. How, then, was the treasure mainly utilised? The traditional answer is hoarding: individuals holding treasure supplies as a form of simple insurance. In an economy lacking modernised local banking networks and continually subject to natural disaster like famine, this clearly made sense for many people. However, as is often remarked [124;149], the practice involved wastage and loss of opportunity for the economy as a whole, particularly since capital shortage was such a fundamental problem. M. Mukherjee estimates that, whilst around 5 per cent of net national income was typically being saved during the late nineteenth century, only about 3 per cent was being committed to investment, the gap indicating the scale of hoarding [22: 75].

We have now, hopefully, reviewed the key factors required for an overall assessment of the foreign trade problem. It seems clear, both from modern measurements of the drain and from the scale of the treasure inflow, that the specific financial demands created by the imperial connection were not, after 1850, excessively burdensome to the Indian economy. On the other hand, the substantial trade surpluses were a source of wasted opportunity, since the advantages of the treasure inflow which ensued were partially dissipated through hoarding. Why, then, was there a chronic trade surplus? One possible answer is a 'vicious circle' in which the poverty of the Indian masses and the relatively slow rate of industrial development consistently limited demand for potentially stimulatory imported products. Many, however, might conclude that an expansionist government response could have dissolved the surplus and hence broken into the vicious circle. If the drain indicates a serious problem, it is, at root, one of conservatism of policy.

5 The State and Economic Development

(i) THE ROOTS OF POLICY

BY raising the issue of government policy, our last chapter's conclusion has pointed us towards one of the most common themes in the historiography of British India. Alleged *laissez-faire* official attitudes and non-interventionist policies are frequently allotted much blame 'for shortcomings of Indian development in the nineteenth century. Thus, even Morris, for all his claims for 'substantial growth', concludes that 'the "night watchman" policies of the state were not sufficient to permit the development . . . of all the fundamental underpinnings of an industrial revolution' [13: *13*].

Undoubtedly many officials, directly influenced by Adam Smith and his successors [133], held to *laissez-faire* beliefs as a fundamental faith. As late as 1910 Morley, the Secretary of State for India in Asquith's Cabinet, refused to sanction the creation of a Department of Industries in Madras to develop government-owned industrial enterprises, on the grounds that such activities should be reserved for private enterprise [137: *226*]. Nevertheless, acceptance that in India, with its intense problems, forms of interventionism unacceptable in Britain were required – a belief which had the authority of J. S. Mill – was also deeply rooted in official thinking. The imperial dimension, too, encouraged for many the vision of reshaping India in the European mould. Thus the social policies of the first half of the nineteenth century, fuelled by Utilitarian political ideologies [131], were unashamedly interventionist, abolishing *sati*, introducing Western concepts of justice and property.

More fundamental, all policy was tightly circumscribed by the basic 'imperial problem'; that a small number of foreigners were attempting to rule a vast, teeming Asian empire. Maintenance of this empire was an unquestioned first principle and this required both some firm recognition of Indian interests and a necessary spirit of activity in the face of security problems. One major example came in agrarian policy. Most officials' inclinations were to create a totally free market in land, permitting, if necessary, social change in the cause of agricultural development. However, the fears raised during the second half of the nineteenth century about massive land transfer and the proletarianisation of peasant proprietors challenged such attitudes and enabled reformers to stress the serious security danger, that a disaffected peasantry might turn to violent protest. Hence a series of interventionist measures – beginning with the Deccan Agriculturists' Relief Act of 1879 [76: *ch. 1*] – attempted to ameliorate peasant indebtedness and inhibit agrarian change. These actions culminated in the Punjab Alienation of Land Act of 1900, which explicitly forbade the sale and mortgage of certain lands to specified non-agriculturist castes. Here was an unabashed attack on the free market principle, but one widely accepted because the security problem of land transfer in the Punjab was intensified both by the Province's religious complexities and its importance as a recruiting ground for the Indian Army.

Government policy was also inevitably pressurised by metropolitan considerations and demands. Business and industrial groups in Britain, particularly the cotton industry, enjoyed an important stake in India and the pursuit of these interests often cut across non-interventionist sentiment. Thus many mid-nineteenth-century Manchester free traders, when considering India, demanded more energetic government action to improve communications and promote agricultural development [120], with the aim of widening sources of raw cotton supply as well as increasing demand for the finished product. Policy was never the simple slave of such pressure groups, but their impact was complex because often mutually contradictory. 'Opening up' the country was not only desired by British interests but also seemed, to nineteenth-century minds, the avenue to Indian development. However, it might threaten not merely *laissez-faire* principles but also the low taxation which Tomlinson calls 'the secret of successful Indian government' [125: *338*].

Further, 'government policy' was never a uniform force. Policy formation after 1858 occurred at three entirely distinct levels: the India Office in London headed by the Secretary of State, a member of the British Cabinet, the central Government of India presided over by the Viceroy and the provincial governments led, normally, by a governor. On particular issues the approaches of these different administrations could and did vary widely, but even they were not simple monoliths. There were frequently disparities of approach between the professional civil servants and the British government nominees who served as Viceroys and governors and also between different departments, notably the judicial and the revenue, within governments. There were, in sum, always 'policies' rather than 'policy'. In the 1910 case quoted earlier, the real situation was that an aggressively *laissez-faire* Secretary of State had temporarily baulked the interventionist party which held sway at Madras.

The complexity of economic policy formation, therefore, should be axiomatic. Even Bhattacharya's characterisation that policy was 'essentially pragmatic' [136: 1] seems over-conceptualisation if it implies some consistent reaction to recognised practical problems. This is not to 'excuse' policy and the policy-makers, for continual subordination to a range of powerful diverse pressures might have amounted to a fatal malaise. Nevertheless, economic policy clearly was likely to vary, fitting ill with non-interventionist stereotypes.

(ii) GOVERNMENT POLICY AND INDUSTRIAL DEVELOPMENT

For many developing economies in the nineteenth century the question of the initiation of railway construction presented the state with the primary test of its attitude to modern industrialisation. Consumer industries were normally the preserve of private initiative, but the beginnings of modern communications required such large capital investment that some state guarantee was often necessary. The Government of India was sufficiently confident of the economic, political and strategic advantages of a railway system, to promote in 1849 a major agreement with the private railway companies, providing substantial aid for their operations. In particular it guaranteed a minimum rate of interest, usually 5 per cent on paid-up capital for ninety-nine years, and the provision of land free of charge [136: 10]. By European standards, such concessions were far from ungenerous and they permitted the development of a basic rail network – connecting the three major ports of Calcutta, Bombay and Madras with Delhi and the Ganges Plain – by 1870. However, the costs of the operation had proved substantial. Profits fell short of the guaranteed rate and the government, therefore, made up the deficit. Crucially, too, during the 1860s the authorities could borrow at interest rates lower than they were guaranteeing to the private companies. By 1870, then, financial logic dictated change and in the following decade considerable activity began on the direct construction of railways by the state.

58

At the peak, in the mid 1870s, the government was spending over £3 million per annum on railway construction [135: *102*]. Thereafter, there were occasional reversions to a private guarantee system at times of financial difficulty, particularly during the late 1870s when the coincidence of famine, the Afghan War of 1878 and the devaluation of the rupee as a consequence of silver's depreciation, created crisis. Even so the state continued to build railways and, from the 1880s, began to buy up privately constructed lines. By 1903 there were 26,851 miles of railway track open in India, over 20,000 miles of which were state-owned [135: *104*]. Finally, during the 1920s, all Indian railways were brought under direct state management.

This, then, represented a substantial state initiative, remembering that funds were borrowed extensively to promote the railways, and one which compares relatively favourably with responses in equivalent late developers. If interventionism remained opposed by some and initially condoned only because of financial problems with the guarantee system, the same, for example, could be said of Russia. Indeed, the Russian government's disillusion with guarantees and its shift to direct state construction, coming during the late 1870s, lagged behind Indian recognition of the most cost-effective policy by about a decade. In Japan – the only Asian country to match the speed of Indian railway construction over the late nineteenth century – the government largely retreated from direct constructional activity during the 1880s and 1890s.[10]

The promotion of railway construction formed part of the Indian government's growing acceptance of its responsibility for public works, after a long period of relative inactivity during the first half of the nineteenth century. In 1854 a separate Government of India Public Works Department was set up with control over construction of roads, bridges and, especially important, irrigation works [136: *4*]. At the same time, the state began operations on a telegraph system: by 1866 over 14,000 miles of line existed [135: *3*]. The major ports were another scene of official activity, the government directly constructing and maintaining harbours, dockyards and lighthouses.

Such basic infrastructural development was, perhaps, by now widely recognised as a state responsibility, but the Indian government's role occasionally went beyond this to direct involvement in pilot industrial projects. In the iron industry, in particular, government founded two concerns during the mid-nineteenth century, the Kumaon Ironworks in 1855–56 and the Burwai Ironworks in

1860–61 [135: *104–13*]. The degree of official commitment here, it should be stressed, was extremely small, the objective being solely the encouragement of private activity in heavy industry. Both works remained under government ownership for only short periods and neither enjoyed any long-term success. Nevertheless, the Government of India's acquisition, in 1882, of the Barakar Ironworks in Bengal, following the failure of its private owners, represented greater involvement. For the next seven years the government ran the works as a profitable enterprise before handing them over as a going concern to the Bengal Iron and Steel Company in 1889. Meanwhile, direct industrial ownership to meet the state's own needs was growing in importance. The state railways, for example, operated their own large engineering workshops which built carriages and did repairs. The government, also, established and ran printing presses – the Central Press at Calcutta was founded in 1863 – army clothing factories and a harness and saddlery factory. Government ordnance factories were particularly important as centres of advanced technology: the first steel bar rolling mill in India, and hence the first modern production of steel in the subcontinent, was inaugurated at an ordnance factory in 1896 [135: *126*].

In sum, as S. K. Sen comments, 'during the second half of the nineteenth century a "public sector" had come into existence' in India [135: *8*]. Indeed, it needs to be emphasised that direct government ownership within the Indian economy in 1900 was no less extensive than in some latecomers to industrialisation, often characterised as stimulated by state-induced growth. In Russia and in Germany government took responsibility for the construction and operation of railways but typically shied away from extensive ownership within the industrial economy. So, too, did the Meiji government in Japan, after its initial direct industrial sponsorship programme of the 1870s; the exception of the state's establishment of the Yawata iron and steel works in the late 1890s is counterbalanced by the Meiji government's construction of only a minority of the country's rail track. There were, however, critical distinctions between official attitudes in India and those in Japan and the European countries. In the latter, government, whilst imposing strict boundaries to its actions, attempted to co-ordinate its measures to promote modernisation and industrial growth. Thus the Russian government, during the Finance Ministership of Witte in the 1890s, pursued a massive programme of railway construction which, linked to high tariffs and the encouragement of foreign investment, considerably stimulated home heavy industry. In India during the nineteenth century there was no consistent developmental dynamic behind official actions, in short no industrial policy as such. Whilst Indian officials were well aware, for example, of the potential multiplier effects of railway construction, Witte's overall perspective – his obsession with speed and his sense of interlocking developmental processes transforming an economy – was entirely lacking.

After 1900, however, changes started to occur. Curzon's Viceroyalty (1899–1905), Dewey comments [137: 219], marked a newly defined commitment to industrial development, and in 1907 a separate Department of Commerce and Industry within the Government of India was created. There was more positive support for private industrial initiatives, marked by active encouragement of the infant Burma Oil industry [140] and substantial aid to the Tatas after the foundation of Jamshedpur. Direct industrial sponsorship particularly arose in Madras, where, under the inspiration of one energetic official, Alfred Chatterton, the government during the first years of the twentieth century successfully founded and ran an aluminium hollow-ware industry, as well as a tanning and weaving factory [135: 131]. Morley's refusal to sanction the Madras Department of Industries in 1910 was obviously a sharp check to these activities but his prohibition was soon rescinded by his successor, Crewe. It was, however, the First World War which seemed to effect the significant shift in attitudes. The report of the Indian Industrial Commission in 1919 firmly supported the concept that government should play an active role in industrial development [137: 216–7]. This foreshadowed substantial policy changes during the 1920s [137] and the expansion of Sen's nineteenth-century 'public sector', so that by 1928, on Clow's estimate, 'close on 10 per cent' of the Indian factory workforce was employed in publicly owned factories [139].

Discussion on the successes and failures of the 'new industrial policy' of the 1920s is beyond our brief here, but we should consider how far the dynamic of policy was really changing after 1900. The innovations of the 1900–1914 period were mainly the work of enthusiasts like Chatterton and groups of activists still regarded sceptically by much of the official establishment. In turn, the Industrial Commission's firm commitment to interventionism arguably owed most to intense problems in the supply of industrial goods and equipment caused by the First World War.

The absence of a co-ordinated government industrial strategy before 1914 was, perhaps, most persistently evident in the field of purchasing policy. As in all less developed countries, the state inevitably played a major role within the economy as a customer generating a significant proportion of the demand for modern industrial products. However, before 1870, whilst purchases of most basic commodities were made locally, orders for much modern equipment were automatically channelled to British industry. Only the devaluation of the rupee against the pound during the 1870s, by markedly increasing the cost of British imports, caused qualms and led to new emphasis during the early 1880s on buying Indian where Indian goods were competitive. Nevertheless, the balance of official purchases did not change radically [135: *ch. 2*]. It was 1901 before Indian firms supplied their first equipment (rolling stock) to the state railways and, despite further relaxations of the 'Stores Rules' in the years immediately before the First World War, expenditure on major 'stores' in Britain by the Government of India continued to exceed equivalent purchases from Indian industry [135: *19,25*]. Of course, it might be claimed that the benefits of high quality imports outweighed the disadvantage of lessened demand for indigenous industry. Again, the large guaranteed orders placed with the Tata Iron and Steel Company in the 1910s did show that government, where it recognised the necessity, was by then prepared to use its purchasing role decisively. Before 1914, however, this degree of support stood as an exception, sharply pointing the loss of opportunities during the nineteenth century. Lehmann [116] argues, as an example, that a powerful Indian locomotive industry might, with more encouragement, have developed. Even during the First World War India did not make the import substitution gains that might have been expected [127: *504*].

Here many would see imperial manipulation to blame: Lehmann points to British exporters' pressure influencing the fixing of standards for locomotives. Equally, however, policy and the administrative structure within India was inert in the face of purchasing opportunities, usually preferring traditional sources. There did not even exist, during the nineteenth century, any special department or agency for the purchase of stores in the Indian market.

(iii) TARIFF AND FINANCIAL POLICY

Imperial pressures, however, undoubtedly had a consistent impact on policy in one crucial area: tariff policy. Fundamentally, as is well known, Indian industry was denied any significant tariff protection throughout the period down to the First World War. On occasions – in 1859–62, the mid 1870s and 1894–96 – Indian governments attempted to raise moderate tariffs [142;143;144;145]. Each time this was a response, not to protectionist sentiment, but to severe short-term financial needs: the costs created by Dalhousie's wars and the Mutiny in 1859–62, the impact of war and famine in the 1870s and the crisis caused by the marked depreciation of the rupee in the mid 1890s. Even under these pressures, however, the policy was overruled and changed from London, largely as a result of fierce and effective lobbying from British interests, notably the Lancashire cotton industry. There was, also, within this structure, a progressive tendency towards free trade. In 1882 the traditional cotton duties were entirely abolished [143: 264] and the outcome of the 1894–96 dispute, whilst preserving a reimposed duty of 3½ per cent, saw the imposition of a countervailing excise on equivalent Indian products [144]. In 1914 India entered the war with a policy 'as close to free trade as any country is likely to have' [127: 501].

Few could deny, then, that here was subordination of Indian to wider imperial needs, providing too a sharp contrast with government policy in continental Europe, where tariff barriers were steadily erected in the era between 1880 and 1914. Ideology also seemed influential here. As we have seen, Indian governments did not advocate positive protection but merely tariffs as a fiscal device, retaining the strong belief in free trade which characterised Britain's own commercial policies in the period. Even so, tariff policy in India is still explicable, as Dewey effectively shows [145], in terms of responses to particular pressures, the typical dynamic of policy. During the late nineteenth century, when British elections might be won and lost in Lancashire, the cotton lobby possessed considerable political leverage within Britain, whilst countervailing influences on the imperial establishment from Indian commercial and industrial groups were still extremely weak. Further, the Indian financial crises which produced demands for higher tariffs were short-term, not structural. All this, however, was to change after the First World War. The political power of Lancashire and Bombay was reversed. The financial situation of Indian governments became more desperate. Tariffs, as a politically popular tax, were now uniquely attractive to the imperial authorities: and hence a rapid and substantial build-up of tariffs, involving much deliberate protection, would occur [146].

But how far did the absence of such protection before 1914 inhibit

Indian development? Undoubtedly both established industries, like cotton, and newly emergent ones, like steel and paper-making, were to grow considerably behind the inter-war tariff wall [82: *chs 7,9,13*]. Tariffs, however, typically imposed costs as well as benefits. They increased the price of goods for the consumer and, unless policy was sufficiently flexible, the price of raw materials for industry. Tariffs in late nineteenth-century continental Europe, for all their vaunted developmental role, were not above committing the latter sin, since many within governments regarded their fiscal value as paramount, or were predominantly concerned with protecting agrarian interests. As a result, some now question whether high tariffs before 1914 would have significantly benefited the Indian economy [14: *171–2*; 138: *13*]. Besides any general reservations about tariffs' utility, imports into India, as we have noted before, were often not directly competing with home production. There is no evidence that the historical shift towards complete free trade during the late nineteenth century directly harmed Indian industry. Farnie, indeed, points out that Indian cotton mills enjoyed boom conditions in the years immediately following the complete abolition of the cotton duties in 1882 [126: *110–1*]. In addition, those sceptical of the potential value of protection to nineteenth-century India can, of course, always point to the example of Meiji Japan, also denied the tariff weapon during the initial stages of modern industrialisation.

Undoubtedly, some counterfactual calculation might well reveal limited direct gain from tariff protection before 1914. This, however, would be to ignore the wider impact protection might have had on the Indian economy. The tariff wall surrounding late nineteenth-century Russia, for example, not only aided home industry in its competition with imports but also encouraged foreign interests, traditional exporters to Russia, to surmount the barrier by directly establishing new enterprises within the country. The substantial inflow of foreign investment, therefore, into late Tsarist Russia was partly a consequence of high tariffs. Would Indian protection have produced similar results? India, whilst lacking the great extractive industries towards which foreign investment in Russia particularly flowed, still boasted, like Russia, a potentially vast home market. On this line of argument, then, the fall-off in the rate of growth of British investment in India after 1870 might well be partly explained by the comparative attractions of protected and unprotected markets.

Alternatively, it might be attributed to inadequacies of monetary and financial policy. Russia in 1897 joined most European countries on a full gold standard regulated by a powerful central bank: in India 'officials had little idea of how to bring this about' [138: *19*]. The Indian monetary system inevitably came under stress with the rapid devaluation of the rupee during the late nineteenth century. In 1893 the Government of India closed the Indian mints as a crisis measure to force up the exchange rate. Thereafter, although official committees in 1893 and 1899 recommended a full gold standard, what emerged, from 1898, was the maintenance of a silver coinage within India together with a 'gold exchange standard' organised from London: as a means of exchange, the India Office sold Council bills for sterling in London which were met by rupee payments in India.

Recent accounts insist on the success of these arrangements in the years immediately before the First World War, in particular for avoiding unnecessary movements of bullion [138: *ch. 1*; 151]. Almost certainly, too, they are correct to absolve the India Office of any deliberate manipulation of Indian currency matters. Nevertheless, the system did show British determination to oversee the continuing evolution of India's monetary system. Noticeably in the inter-war period, whilst Indian governments acquired unchallenged control over tariff policy, London periodically reimposed a decisive influence over the exchange rate of the rupee, particularly asserted during the crisis of 1931 [152]. More important, the system, whilst working relatively smoothly between 1898 and 1914, was still vulnerable to sharp fluctuations in the value of silver, because of the maintenance of a silver currency: the marked rise in silver's value after 1916, by threatening to push the bullion value of coins above their exchange value, necessitated a swift rise in the rupee [150;151].

These, however, were perhaps inevitable problems. The fundamental drawback of the Indian system was that it did not require or produce a fully fledged central bank, with power of note issue or control over the money market: that only emerged with the establishment of the Reserve Bank of India in 1935 [138: *128–131*]. This shortcoming not only underpinned the disaggregation of the banking network but also its inflexibility, for a central bank might have facilitated the practical working of the commercial system through supply of short-term credits. There is much, then, to be said for Keynes's conclusion in 1913 that, whilst India's gold exchange standard was 'in the forefront of monetary progress', 'in her banking arrangements, in the management of her note issue, and in the relations of her Government to the Money Market, her position *is* anomalous and she has much to learn . . .' [147: *259*].

(iv) THE STATE AND DEVELOPMENT IN INDIA

The British Indian state, in the period down to 1914, undoubtedly acted as a predominantly conservative force within the economy: this was the institution which could knowingly preside over a large foreign trade surplus. Much expenditure was generally unproductive economically. Defence spending was always high, monopolising up to 30 per cent of total expenditure in the period 1870–1900 [141: *471*]. Clearly this had productive multiplier effects – demand for arsenals, and for uniforms from textile industries – but in India these were circumscribed by equipment purchases abroad. At the same time, the structure of revenue raising was regressive. The land revenue provided around half of the gross revenue for most of the first half of the nineteenth century and even in 1900 was by far the leading single tax, producing about 40 per cent of taxation revenue. Taxes on items of mass consumption, notably the salt tax, were also substantial revenue raisers. In contrast, income tax was only introduced in 1886, to be followed by a stamp tax on businesses, but their contribution was scanty before 1914. Once more, though, Indian practice was hardly unique. European administrations devoted large proportions of their expenditure to defence, particularly in the 1870–1914 era, and even the Russian government of the 1890s spent a small proportion of its overall resources on constructive projects. Again, if Indian government taxed the peasantry to obtain much of its revenue, so too did the Meiji administration in Japan, at any rate in the 1870s and 1880s. One could, indeed, argue that this stimulated nascent business and industrial activity by limiting the taxation burden which it bore.

This comparative dimension has recently given rise, as Jones comments [140], to a powerful revisionism within the literature on the state's role. Direct comparisons – notably, as we saw, on the degree of ownership within the nineteenth-century economy – by no means demonstrate Indian government activity in an unfavourable light. However, the new revisionism may be running too far if, in Jones's terms, it sees Indian government policy as entirely consistent with that in Europe except for the existence of 'several substantial "blemishes"' [140: *354*]. Whilst areas such as tariff policy might be regarded simply as 'blemishes' with possibly limited consequences, there was, more fundamentally, a clear absence of any strong developmental thrust generated by the nineteenth-century Indian state. This is not to say that its existence would have revolutionised India's economic situation. As with the foreign trade sector, there are questions about the scale of any contribution or deficiency created by government policy: Dewey makes a powerful plea for questioning the importance of the state's constructive role in the industrialisation of latecomers [137: *249*]. Nevertheless, the broad intellectual tradition which stretches from List to Gerschenkron as well as the experience of individual economies like Russia in the 1890s does suggest that a carefully structured government strategy could help to overcome backwardness in the nineteenth century.

However, if we are to regard Indian policy as, in some way, deficient, we need to be clear about the nature of the deficiency. Nineteenth-century critics of British rule fulminated against an allegedly all-powerful imperialism, bleeding India of her wealth. Nevertheless, the picture which emerges from our study is of government policy closely confined by pressures and with strictly limited room for manoeuvre: in view of the forces exerted on Indian governments, it is hard to see how tariff and monetary policy, for example, could have been radically different. The weakness of the imperial policy-makers is perhaps best illustrated by their fiscal resources. The real significance of the prominence of land revenue in the nineteenth century is arguably that such fiscal devices were less flexible and capable of steady expansion than taxes on incomes and customs duties. Whilst there is no definitive modern work on the taxation burden, it seems unlikely that, after the tight land revenue squeeze of the early nineteenth century, it grew much in real terms down to 1914. Receipts from the opium monopoly fell steadily away and there was no great new fiscal source until the explosion in customs duties during and after the First World War. Maddison has estimated that even in 1936 total collections of central and provincial taxes amounted to about 6·6 per cent of GNP, around a third of equivalent proportions in contemporary Western economies [19: *48*]. Indian development, on this argument, was inhibited not by exploitative overtaxation but by undertaxation and consequent government inability to play an energetic stimulatory role.

6 · Conclusions

WITHIN our sectoral review, can we decipher any common historical trends in the Indian economy's evolution? One might argue that conditions for development were at their most favourable over the second half of the nineteenth century. Foreign capital was attracted into the country, large-scale public works, notably railways, were constructed, and agriculture was able to diversify and respond to international demand without, almost certainly, producing any aggregate deterioration in per capita production of foodgrains. Particularly during the 1860s – when the American Civil War cotton boom coincided with an expansion in public works construction – and again during the run of good harvests between 1880 and 1895 the economy may have been advancing on a wide front. Again, despite the virulence of late nineteenth-century debates, any expropriatory dimension of British rule may now have been moderated. Modern measurement of the then existing 'drain' as comparatively small confirms the view that the fundamental impact of imperial rule on the indigenous economy must have come in the field of revenue raising. Here the 'burden' of imperialism was after 1850 almost certainly less than in the first third of the nineteenth century, when the pumping out of land revenue may have markedly depressed the agricultural economy. The imperialist state was always at its most 'exploitative' during its early stages.

Nevertheless, during the second half of the nineteenth century, the state remained uncommitted to an industrialisation policy. The reasons for this, as we have seen, were more complex than simple ideology and, in any case, the generally favoured strategy of development through agricultural export had much international example to recommend it. However, it seems clear that important opportunities for promoting Indian industrialisation – notably through purchasing policy – were squandered. Alternatively, remembering the trading position, government might have promoted purchase of capital goods and equipment abroad much more extensively and constructively without threatening economic stability.

Even so, India's growing industrial exports were unlucky to encounter in Asian markets, by the close of the nineteenth century, an aggressively competitive rival. It was always likely that Asia, with its highly developed agriculture, mass markets and sophisticated civilisation, would support one spontaneous industrial revolution on the British model. Yet its emergence in Japan from the late nineteenth century – like the British 'lead' established between 1780 and 1815 – immediately made conditions more difficult for competitors.

The problem, then, of timing – of various stimulants to industrialisation coming together at one period in a self-sustaining manner – may have been a serious obstacle to Indian development. Lamb makes essentially the same point for the 1920s when she argues that the 'new industrial policy' then came simply too late [134: *484*]. Linked to major infrastructural developments, its spin-offs might have been considerable, but by the 1920s the initial impetus of major public works construction was lost and the rate of new foreign capital inflow diminished radically. Such chronological dislocations, as we have seen, are equally evident before 1914. One might argue that, if an economy so backward as India's was to experience substantial development, a highly convenient historical conjunction of stimulatory forces was probably necessary. This never occurred during the British period.

But what was the role of the imperial impact? The new tendency to emphasise the weakness and limitations of imperialism would suggest that India's problem was that foreign modernising impulses were not strong and intrusive enough rather than that they were devastatingly destructive. It is possible, of course, that the mixture which occurred was the worst of all worlds: that imperialism had very limited impact on the grass-roots economy whilst still building at the margin an expropriatory mechanism capable of pumping out funds. However, the scale of any expropriatory force arising out of external relationships, as modern discussion of the drain has shown, must have been relatively small. This is a finding of relevance, arguably, beyond India. It also reasserts the crucial point about the scale of importance of different sectors of the economy. Even if, on our argument, agriculture was subject to greater growth and diversification than is commonly assumed, the performance of the agricultural sector may still stand, because of its vast size and contribution to the national product, as the overwhelming impediment to Indian development.

Questions of scale, when related to the imperial impact, are also revealing in other directions. As we have seen, foreign capital dominated investment in the modern sector during the nineteenth century and yet, in per capita terms, the volume of foreign investment in India remained, relatively, tiny. This clearly suggests an economy facing widespread capital shortage in the quest for industrial development. The state, in turn, was too weak to attempt to change the situation. This is not to absolve the imperial government of criticism. One major reason why it failed to evolve a wider fiscal base during the nineteenth century was because imperialism's necessary obsessions with its own security required low taxation and traditional fiscal forms. Imperial rulers were timid rulers: the real problem of the drain was not the actual outflow involved but the conservatism of policy in ensuring a large margin beyond meeting it. The British Raj, too, inevitably lacked the sense of national identity, and the appearance of national consent, necessary for the successful pursuit of a state-sponsored development push. In these areas lay, perhaps, the real curse of imperialism.

Even an independent government actively pursuing rapid industrialisation would, however, have been no guarantee of a better developmental performance. One might reasonably conclude that the Japanese state over the period 1870–1914 was more successful in promoting industrialisation, although policy here, too, undoubtedly had its limitations and costs. Japan, however, had enjoyed certain crucial advantages over India in 1800: in terms of social stability, in the capacity of the political authorities to raise taxation revenue, even in levels of mass literacy. In the Indian case, without this legacy, any governmental drive to industrialisation in the nineteenth century might well have imposed massive social costs on the population. The industrialisation strategy promoted by the government of late Tsarist Russia, whatever its economic impact, was ultimately self-defeating in social and political terms. By providing the economic muscle to wage international war and by seeming to develop at the expense of, rather than to the benefit of, mass living standards, it helped eventually to destroy the regime. Ray comments of the inter-war period of the twentieth century: 'only savage, single-minded determination and will-power, that brooked no obstacle or resistance . . . could have carried the Indian economy forward at a pace comparable to that of Japan or Russia' [83: 234]. This might equally be said of the century before 1914, remembering that Indian industrialisation in the period was inevitably constrained by severe problems of demand in a poor economy.

Some of the historical problems of India's economic development might, in conclusion, be further highlighted by models developed to explain European industrialisation, a source hitherto largely neglected by economic historians of the Third World. Gerschenkron's well-known concept of 'backwardness', for example, purports to explain how industrial development occurred in nineteenth-century continental Europe through the emergence of special institutional arrangements – notably joint-stock banks or state activity – designed to overcome the country's backwardness relative to the British pioneer.[11] Whatever the merits and deficiencies of Gerschenkron's idea, it is immediately clear that India, although manifestly very 'backward' by these standards, was hardly capable of this type of development. The state was too weak financially and the modern banking system was highly enclavist. No special dynamic institutions, except the foreign innovation of the managing agency, emerged in nineteenth-century India to overcome backwardness. But why was this? Obviously the scale of India's economic backwardness can be largely blamed. But, strikingly, Gerschenkron's model also presupposes a political and military drive within state and society to industrialise in order to compete effectively with neighbouring rivals. Imperialism – the existence of a foreign government – and the absence of a strong national identity robbed India of this drive, but so, too, did the political atmosphere of nineteenth-century South Asia, in which a stable civilisation like British-ruled India lacked any fundamental threat to its position. The coincidence of a more determined industrialisation drive after 1914 with a world war and with the emergence of Japanese power may be significant. Industrialisation in nineteenth-century Europe was clearly often an off-shoot of the quest for political power and status in a highly competitive national situation. In nineteenth-century India the political as well as economic framework for rapid industrial development was essentially lacking.

Notes and References

Unless otherwise indicated, London is the place of publication.

1. As an entrée to the literature on such concepts, see André Gunder Frank, *Capitalism and Underdevelopment in Latin America* (New York, 1967) and *Dependent Accumulation and Underdevelopment* (1978); Immanuel Wallerstein, *The Capitalist World-Economy* (Cambridge, 1979).

2. All the detailed discussion in this work will be based on British India. However, major research by economic historians on the princely states is at last starting to emerge. See, in particular, Bjorn Hettne, *The Political Economy of Indirect Rule: Mysore, 1881–1947* (1978) and the debate between John Hurd and C. P. Simmons and B. R. Satyanarayana in *The Indian Economic and Social History Review*, 12, 2 (April 1975) and 16, 2 (April–June 1979).

3. This and later unsupported statistical material is taken from the appropriate *Statistical Abstract of British India* published annually in *Parliamentary Papers*: an easily accessible source of basic data for the economic historian.

4. Braudel's illuminating discussion of rice cultivation can be read in Fernand Braudel, *Capitalism and Material Life 1400–1800* (1974) pp. 97–108.

5. For the salient details of the Japanese debate, see James I. Nakamura, *Agricultural Production and the Economic Development of Japan, 1873–1922* (Princeton, 1966); H. Rosovsky, 'Rumbles in the Ricefields: Professor Nakamura v the Official Statistics', *Journal of Asian Studies*, 27 (February 1968) 347–60; K. Ohkawa, B. Johnston and H. Kaneda (eds), *Agriculture and Economic Growth: Japan's Experience* (Princeton, 1970).

6. A recent debate between Alan Heston and Ashok Desai seems to leave this point firmly established. See *The Indian Economic and Social History Review*, 15, 2 (April–June 1978) 173–210.

7. See, for example, S. B. Hanley and Kozo Yamamura, *Economic and Demographic Change in Preindustrial Japan, 1600–1868* (Princeton, 1977).

8. This is certainly true of the pre-industrial West. For a recent discussion of the ubiquity of rural credit in early modern England,

see B. A. Holderness, 'Credit in English Rural Society before the Nineteenth Century, with Special Reference to the Period 1605–1720', *Agricultural History Review*, 24, (1976) 97–109.

9. This point about the early impact of British rule has been well made and developed in an as yet unpublished paper by Professor Eric Stokes, 'Bentinck to Dalhousie: The Rationale of Indian Empire'. I am very grateful to Professor Stokes, who allowed me to consult this paper.

10. The comparison with policy in Russia and Japan is clearly a useful one for India. On Russia, see especially T. H. Von Laue, *Sergei Witte and the Industrialisation of Russia* (New York, 1963); Arcadius Kahan, 'Government Policies and the Industrialisation of Russia', *Journal of Economic History*, 27, (December 1967) 460–77; J. P. McKay, *Pioneers For Profit: Foreign Entrepreneurship and Russian Industrialisation, 1885–1913* (Chicago, 1970); Malcolm Falkus, 'Aspects of Foreign Investment in Tsarist Russia', *Journal of European Economic History*, 8, 1 (Spring 1979) 5–36. On Japan, see especially W. W. Lockwood, *The Economic Development of Japan* (Princeton, 1954) ch. 10; H. T. Oshima 'Meiji Fiscal Policy and Economic Progress', ch. 8 of W. W. Lockwood (ed.), *The State and Economic Enterprise in Japan* (Princeton, 1965); B. K. Marshall, *Capitalism and Nationalism in Pre-War Japan* (Stanford, 1967); I. Inukai and A. Tussing, 'Kogyo Iken: Japan's Ten Year Plan, 1884', *Economic Development and Cultural Change*, 16, (1967–68) pp. 51–71; Kozo Yamamura, 'Entrepreneurship, Ownership and Management in Japan', M. M. Postan and Peter Mathias (eds), *The Cambridge Economic History*, vol. 7, part 2 (Cambridge, 1978) pp. 215–64.

11. See Alexander Gerschenkron, *Economic Backwardness in Historical Perspective* (Cambridge Mass., 1962). Professor Cyril Ehrlich has recently suggested the utility, for Third World economic history, of examining such models.

Select Bibliography

The literature on the economic history of India is extensive and rapidly growing. The sources given here are those cited in the text together with a few additions which may be of aid in further reading on particular issues. The bibliography is arranged into sections to correspond, so far as possible, with the divisions of subject-matter in the text. Unless otherwise indicated, the place of publication is London. The following abbreviations are used:

EHR:	*Economic History Review*, Second Series
EEH:	*Explorations in Economic History*
IESHR:	*The Indian Economic and Social History Review*
JAS:	*Journal of Asian Studies*
MAS:	*Modern Asian Studies*
Economy and Society:	K. N. Chaudhuri and C. J. Dewey (eds), *Economy and Society. Essays in Indian Economic and Social History* (New Delhi, 1979)
Imperial Impact:	C. J. Dewey and A. G. Hopkins (eds), *The Imperial Impact. Studies in the Economic History of Africa and India* (1978)

GENERAL SOURCES

(i) The 'Classics' of Indian economic history

The works of Naoroji, Dutt and Digby form the leading contemporary criticisms of the economic effects of British rule. Griffiths, in contrast, provides a major example of the 'diffusionist' approach, stressing the constructive role of the imperial impact. Avineri's collection includes Marx's main articles on the Indian economy.

[1] Dadabhai Naoroji, *Poverty and UnBritish Rule in India* (1871).

[2] Romesh Dutt, *The Economic History of India in the Victorian Age from the Accession of Queen Victoria in 1837 to the Commencement of the Twentieth Century* (8th impression, 1956).

[3] W. Digby, *'Prosperous' British India* (1901).

[4] Sir Percival Griffiths, *The British Impact on India* (1952).

[5] Shlomo Avineri, *Karl Marx on Colonialism and Modernisation* (New York, 1969), pp. 88–95, 99–108, 132–9, 235–9, 330–5.

(ii) Modern Bibliographical Surveys

Morris and Stein and Kumar survey the literature to date extensively, whilst Cornish comments on the pre-British background. Divekar provides a comprehensive list of printed material, including government records.

[6] V. D. Divekar (ed.), *Annotated Bibliography on the Economic History of India 1500–1947*, 4 vols (Calcutta, 1977–9).

[7] M. D. Morris and B. Stein, 'The Economic History of India: A Bibliographic Essay', *JEH*, 21, 2 (June 1961) 179–207.

[8] Dharma Kumar, 'Recent Research in the Economic History of Modern India', *IESHR*, 9, 1 (March 1972) 63–90.

[9] Selwyn Cornish, 'Recent Writing in Indian Economic History', *JEH*, 37, 3 (September 1977) 762–6.

[10] M. D. Morris, 'Quantitative Resources for the Study of Indian History', Val R. Lorwin and Jacob M. Price (eds), *The Dimensions of the Past. Materials, Problems and Opportunities for Quantitative Work in History* (New Haven, 1972) pp. 531–49.

(iii) Modern General Studies

The sources given here are at different levels of generality. The books by Maddison and Chamberlain contain acceptable brief introductions. Those by Anstey, Gadgil and Buchanan are still useful, traditional studies. The symposium edited by Morris *et al*, is an important modern debate about the fundamental themes, whilst Macpherson's article ranges widely over the specialist issues. The Thorners' work has been important in unravelling long-term trends.

[11] Angus Maddison, *Class Structure and Economic Growth. India and Pakistan since the Moghuls* (1971), ch. 3.

[12] M. E. Chamberlain, *Britain and India: the Interaction of Two Peoples* (Newton Abbot, 1974), ch. 4.

[13] M. D. Morris, T. Matsui, B. Chandra and T. Raychaudhuri, *The Indian Economy in the Nineteenth Century: a Symposium* (New Delhi, 1969).

[14] W. J. Macpherson, 'Economic Development in India under the British Crown, 1858–1947', A. J. Youngson (ed.), *Economic Development in the Long Run* (1972) pp. 126–91.

[15] Vera Anstey, *The Economic Development of India*, 3rd edn (1957).

[16] D. R. Gadgil, *The Industrial Evolution of India in Recent Times* (Oxford, 1944).

[17] D. H. Buchanan *The Development of Capitalist Enterprise in India*, 2nd edn (1966).

[18] Brian Davey, *The Economic Development of India. A Marxist Analysis* (Nottingham, 1975).

[19] Angus Maddison, 'The Historical Origins of Indian Poverty', *Banca Nazionale del Lavoro Quarterly Review*, 23, 92 (March 1970) 31–81.

[20] Daniel and Alice Thorner, *Land and Labour in India* (1962).

[21] Daniel Thorner, 'Long-term Trends in Output in India', Simon Kuznets, Wilbert E. Moore and Joseph J. Spengler (eds), *Economic Growth: Brazil, India, Japan* (Durham, N. C., 1955) pp. 103–28.

[22] M. Mukherjee, *National Income of India: Trends and Structure* (Calcutta, 1969).

[23] Russell Lidman and Robert I. Domrese, 'India', W. Arthur Lewis (ed.), *Tropical Development 1880–1913* (1970) pp. 309–36.

[24] M. D. Morris, 'Introduction to a Symposium on Indian Economic History', *EEH*, 12, (1975) 253–61.

[25] Victor Kiernan, 'Marx and India', ch. 5 of his *Marxism and Imperialism* (1974).

AGRICULTURE AND THE RURAL ECONOMY

(i) Agriculture: Overall Trends

Blyn's presentation of the agricultural statistics has recently provoked widespread criticism of their accuracy, particularly from

Heston and Dewey. Most modern research attempts to analyse agriculture at provincial level, revealing significant variation in performance.

[26] George Blyn, *Agricultural Trends in India, 1891–1947: Output, Availability and Productivity* (Philadelphia, 1966).

[27] Clive Dewey, 'Patwari and Chaukidar: Subordinate Officials and the Reliability of India's Agricultural Statistics', *Imperial Impact*, pp. 280–314.

[28] Alan W. Heston, 'Official Yields Per Acre in India, 1886–1947: Some Questions of Interpretation', *IESHR*, 10, 4 (December 1973) 303–32.

[29] Ashok V. Desai, 'Revenue Administration and Agricultural Statistics in Bombay Presidency', *IESHR*, 15, 2 (April–June 1978) 173–85.

[30] Alan W. Heston, 'A Further Critique of Historical Yields Per Acre in India', *IESHR*, 15, 2 (April–June 1978) 187–210.

[31] M. D. Morris, 'Economic Change and Agriculture in Nineteenth Century India', *IESHR*, 3, 2 (June 1966) 185–209.

[32] B. H. Farmer, *Agricultural Colonization in India since Independence* (1974).

[33] Rajat Ray, 'The Crisis of Bengal Agriculture 1870–1927: The Dynamics of Immobility', *IESHR*, 10, 3 (September 1973) 244–79.

[34] Ira Klein, 'Population and Agriculture in Northern India, 1872–1971', *MAS*, 8, 2 (April 1974) 191–216.

[35] M. M. Islam, *Bengal Agriculture 1920–1946: A Quantitative Study* (Cambridge, 1978).

[36] Neil Charlesworth, 'Trends in the Agricultural Performance of an Indian Province: the Bombay Presidency, 1900–1920', *Economy and Society*, pp. 113–40.

[37] Amalendu Guha, 'A Big Push Without a Take-off: A Case Study of Assam, 1871–1901', *IESHR*, 5, 3 (September 1968) 199–221.

[38] Peter Harnetty, 'Crop Trends in the Central Provinces of India, 1861–1921', *MAS*, 11, 3 (July 1977) 341–77.

(ii) Population, Food Supply and the Famine Problem

Davis's work, with some refinements by Das Gupta and Morris, provides basic information on demographic trends. Bhatia stresses the prevalence of famine over the second half of the nineteenth century and Klein the generally high mortality, but McAlpin detects a trend towards amelioration by 1900.

[39] Kingsley Davis, *The Population of India and Pakistan* (Princeton, 1951).
[40] Ajit Das Gupta, 'Study of the Historical Demography of India', D. V. Glass and Roger Revelle (eds), *Population and Social Change* (1972) pp. 419–35.
[41] M. D. Morris, 'The Population of All-India, 1800–1951', *IESHR*, 11, 2–3 (June–September 1974) 309–13.
[42] B. M. Bhatia, *Famines in India. A Study in Some Aspects of the Economic History of India, 1860–1945* (1967).
[43] Ira Klein, 'Death in India', *JAS*, 32, 4 (August 1973) 639–59.
[44] M. B. McAlpin, 'Death, Famine and Risk: The Changing Impact of Crop Failures in Western India, 1870–1920', *JEH*, 39, 1 (March 1979) 143–57.

(iii) Agriculture: The Extent and Impact of Commercialisation

Peasant responsiveness to price incentives has been stressed by Harnetty and Narain, but the effects of extending commercial production are widely debated. Whitcombe, for example, argues that large canal irrigation schemes frequently created ecological decline, though Stone challenges this. McAlpin is a meliorist here, too, seeing a much broader distribution of income from cotton production by around 1900. The developmental implications of the credit and debt system are a subject of recent discussion.

[45] Peter Harnetty, 'Cotton Exports and Indian Agriculture, 1861–1870', *EHR*, 24, 3 (August 1971) 414–29.
[46] Dharm Narain, *The Impact of Price Movements on Areas under Selected Crops in India, 1900–1939* (Cambridge, 1965).
[47] M. B. McAlpin, 'Railroads, Cultivation Patterns and Food-grain Availability: India, 1860–1900', *IESHR*, 12, 1 (January–March 1975) 43–60.
[48] ——————, 'The Effects of Expansion of Markets on Rural Income Distribution in Nineteenth Century India', *EEH*, 12, (1975) 289–302.
[49] ——————, 'Railroads, Prices and Peasant Rationality: India, 1860–1900', *JEH*, 34, 3 (September 1974) 662–84.

[50] E. Whitcombe, *Agrarian Conditions in Northern India. Vol 1. The United Provinces under British Rule 1860–1900* (Los Angeles and Berkeley, 1972).

[51] Ian Stone, 'Canal Irrigation and Agrarian Change: The Experience of the Ganges Canal Tract, 1840–1900', *Economy and Society*, pp. 86–112.

[52] David Washbrook, 'Economic Development and Social Stratification in Rural Madras: The "Dry Region", 1878–1929', *Imperial Impact*, pp. 68–82.

[53] Neil Charlesworth, 'Rich Peasants and Poor Peasants in Late Nineteenth Century Maharashtra', *Imperial Impact*, pp. 97–113.

[54] P. J. Musgrave, 'Rural Credit and Rural Society in the United Provinces, 1860–1920', *Imperial Impact*, pp. 216–32.

[55] B. B. Chaudhuri, 'The Growth of Commercial Agriculture and its Impact on the Peasant Economy', *IESHR*, 7, 1 (March 1970) 25–60; 7, 2 (June 1970) 211–51.

[56] John Hurd II, 'Railways and the Expansion of Markets in India, 1861–1921', *EEH*, 12, (1975) 263–88.

[57] Barry H. Michie, 'Baniyas in the Indian Agrarian Economy: A Case of Stagnant Entrepreneurship', *JAS*, 37, 4 (August 1978) 637–52.

(iv) The Land and the Impact of British Policy to 1850

From an initial concern with the motivation behind British revenue policy and its impact, historians have now shifted to more detailed examination of the local agrarian situation and its evolution. Frykenberg's work has especially helped to promote this approach.

[58] Hiroshi Fukazawa, 'Land and Peasants in the Eighteenth Century Maratha Kingdom', *Hitotsubashi Journal of Economics*, 6, 1 (June 1965) 32–61.

[59] Ranajit Guha, *A Rule of Property for Bengal. An Essay on the Idea of Permanent Settlement* (Paris, 1963).

[60] T. H. Beaglehole, *Thomas Munro and the Development of Administrative Policy in Madras, 1792–1818. The Origins of 'the Munro System'* (Cambridge, 1966).

[61] R. E. Frykenberg, *Guntur District 1788–1848: A History of Local Influence and Central Authority in South India* (Oxford, 1965).

[62] Thomas R. Metcalf, *Land, Landlords and the British Raj: Northern India in the Nineteenth Century* (Berkeley and Los Angeles, 1979).

[63] R. E. Frykenberg (ed.), *Land Control and Social Structure in Indian History* (Madison, 1969).

[64] ——————, *Land Tenure and Peasant in South Asia* (New Delhi, 1977).

(v) Social Stability and Change on the Land, 1850–1914

This has always been an area of intense and detailed debate since Darling's day, and only the most prominent material can be given here. In general, modern revisions, particularly pioneered by Stokes and Dharma Kumar, have amended traditional assumptions about extensive social change on the land.

[65] Malcolm Darling, *The Punjab Peasant in Prosperity and Debt* (Clive Dewey (ed.), New Delhi, 1977).

[66] Eric Stokes, *The Peasant and the Raj. Studies in Agrarian Society and Peasant Rebellion in Colonial India* (Cambridge, 1978), especially chs 1, 9 and 12.

[67] Dharma Kumar, 'Landownership and Equality in Madras Presidency 1853/4–1946/7', *IESHR*, 12, 3 (July–September 1975) 229–61.

[68] Tom G. Kessinger, *Vilyatpur 1848–1968: Social and Economic Change in a North Indian Village* (1974).

[69] Walter C. Neale, *Economic Change in Rural India: Land Tenure and Reform in the U.P.* (New Haven, Conn., 1962).

[70] Barrington Moore Jnr, *Social Origins of Dictatorship and Democracy. Lord and Peasant in the Making of the Modern World* (1967), ch. 6.

[71] Surendra J. Patel, *Agricultural Labourers in Modern India and Pakistan* (Bombay, 1952).

[72] Dharma Kumar, *Land and Caste in South India. Agricultural Labour in the Madras Presidency* (Cambridge, 1965).

[73] J. Krishnamurty, 'The Growth of Agricultural Labour in India – A Note', *IESHR*, 9, 3 (September 1972) 327–32.

[74] Jan Breman, *Patronage and Exploitation: Changing Agrarian Relations in South Gujarat, India* (Los Angeles and Berkeley, 1974).

[75] Ravinder Kumar, *Western India in the Nineteenth Century* (1968).
[76] I. J. Catanach, *Rural Credit in Western India. Rural Credit and the Cooperative Movement in the Bombay Presidency 1875–1930* (Los Angeles and Berkeley, 1970).
[77] P. J. Musgrave, 'Social Power and Social Change in the United Provinces 1860–1920', *Economy and Society*, pp. 3–25.

BUSINESS AND INDUSTRY

(i) The Historical Pattern of Industrial Development

Besides the Thorners' important work [20], Bagchi and Krishnamurty have recently made significant contributions to the 'de-industrialisation' debate. Bagchi and Ray's books provide modern studies of industrial development in the twentieth century.

[78] A. K. Bagchi, 'De-industrialisation in India in the Nineteenth Century; Some Theoretical Implications', *Journal of Development Studies*, 12, 2 (January 1976) 135–64.
[79] Marika Vicziany, 'The De-industrialization of India in the Nineteenth Century: A Methodological Critique of Amiya Kumar Bagchi', *IESHR*, 16, 2 (April–June 1979) 105–46.
[80] J. Krishnamurty, 'The Distribution of the Indian Working Force, 1901–1951', *Economy and Society*, pp. 258–76.
[81] Meghnad Desai, 'Demand for Cotton Textiles in Nineteenth Century India', *IESHR*, 8, 4 (December 1971) 337–61.
[82] A. K. Bagchi, *Private Investment in India, 1900–1939* (Cambridge, 1972).
[83] Rajat K. Ray, *Industrialisation in India. Growth and Conflict in the Private Corporate Sector 1914–1947* (Delhi, 1979).
[84] S. J. Koh, *Stages of Industrial Development in Asia. A Comparative History of the Cotton Industry in Japan, India, China and Korea* (Philadelphia, 1966).
[85] A. B. Ghosh, 'India's Foreign Trade in Coal before Independence – A Note', *IESHR*, 6, 4 (December 1969) 437.

(ii) Industrial Structure and Organisation

Rungta's is the major modern study of nineteenth-century business organisation.

[86] R. S. Rungta, *The Rise of Business Corporations in India 1851–1900* (Cambridge, 1970).

[87] B. B. Kling, 'The Origin of the Managing Agents in India', *JAS*, 26, 1 (November 1966) 37–47.

[88] C. P. Simmons, 'Vertical Integration and the Indian Steel Industry. The Colliery Establishment of the Tata Iron and Steel Co., 1907–1956', *MAS*, 11, 1 (February 1977) 127–48.

(iii) Indigenous Business and Entrepreneurship

The old debate about indigenous entrepreneurship has now been given greater depth by a wide range of modern studies of businesses and the merchant ethic and attitudes.

[89] B. B. Misra, *The Indian Middle Classes* (Oxford, 1961).

[90] A. K. Bagchi, 'European and Indian Entrepreneurship in India, 1900–1930', E. Leach and S. N. Mukherjee (eds), *Elites in South Asia* (Cambridge, 1970) pp. 223–56.

[91] Helen Lamb, 'The Indian Merchant', Milton Singer (ed.), *Traditional India: Structure and Change* (Philadelphia, 1959) pp. 25–34.

[92] Kenneth Gillion, *Ahmedabad: A Study in Indian Urban History* (Berkeley, 1968).

[93] C. A. Bayly, 'Indian Merchants in a "Traditional" Setting: Benares, 1780–1830', *Imperial Impact*, pp. 171–93.

[94] T. A. Timberg, 'A North Indian Firm As Seen Through Its Business Records, 1860–1914: Tarachand Ghanshyandas, a Great Marwari Firm', *IESHR*, 8, 3 (September 1971) 264–83.

[95] ——————, 'Three Types of the Marwari Firm', *IESHR*, 10, 1 (March 1973) 1–36.

[96] Marika Vicziany, 'Bombay Merchants and Structural Changes in the Export Community 1850–1880', *Economy and Society*, pp. 163–96.

[97] A. D. Gordon, 'Businessmen and Politics in a Developing Colonial Economy: Bombay City, 1918–1933', *Imperial Impact*, pp. 194–215.

[98] C. P. Simmons, 'Indigenous Enterprise in the Indian Coalmining Industry *c.* 1835–1939', *IESHR*, 13, 2 (April–June 1976) 189–218.

(iv) Social Values and Business Activity

The Weberian tradition has aroused little response among modern economic and social historians, although Morris has recently attempted to broaden the discussion by highlighting the varying ways different groups perceive entrepreneurial opportunity.

[99] Max Weber, *The Religion of India. The Sociology of Hinduism and Buddhism*, Hans H. Gerth and Don Martindale trans. (New York, 1958).

[100] M. D. Morris, 'Values as an Obstacle to Economic Growth in South Asia: An Historical Survey', *JEH*, 27, 4 (December 1967) 588–607.

[101] Kingsley Davis, 'Social and Demographic Aspects of Economic Development in India', Simon Kuznets, Wilbert E. Moore and Joseph J. Spengler (eds), *Economic Growth: Brazil, India, Japan* (Durham N.C., 1955), pp. 263–315.

[102] M. D. Morris, 'South Asian Entrepreneurship and the Rashomon Effect, 1800–1947', *EEH*, 16, 3 (July 1979) 341–61.

(v) Labour Supply to Industry

This has become much the most heavily investigated issue arising from questions of social response to industrialisation: a number of accounts have developed the themes established in Morris's pioneer account of the Bombay mills.

[103] M. D. Morris, *The Emergence of an Industrial Labour Force in India: A Study of the Bombay Cotton Mills, 1854–1947* (Berkeley, 1965).

[104] D. Mazumdar, 'Labour Supply in Early Industrialisation: the Case of the Bombay Textile Industry', *EHR*, 26, 3 (August 1973) 477–96.

[105] R. K. Newman, 'Social Factors in the Recruitment of the Bombay Millhands', *Economy and Society*, pp. 277–95.

[106] Baniprasanna Misra, 'Factory Labour during the Early Years of Industrialisation: An Appraisal in the Light of the Indian Factory Commission, 1890', *IESHR*, 12, 3 (July 1975) 203–28.

[107] Ranajit Das Gupta, 'Factory Labour in Eastern India: Sources of Supply, 1855–1946, Some Preliminary Findings', *IESHR*, 13, 3 (July–September 1976) 277–329.

[108] Lalita Chakravarty, 'The Emergence of an Industrial Labour Force in a Dual Economy – British India, 1880–1920', *IESHR*, 15, 3 (July–September 1978) 249–328.

[109] E. A. Ramaswamy, 'Trade Unionism and Caste in South India', *MAS*, 10, 3 (July 1976) 361–73.

INVESTMENT, TRADE AND THE IMPERIAL CONNECTION

(i) Foreign Investment in India

Jenks is still very useful as a general source, whilst Kidron and Tomlinson provide modern surveys of trends of a later period. Much specialist investigation has concentrated on the railways, as the prime recipient of foreign capital.

[110] Leland H. Jenks, *The Migration of British Capital to 1875* (1963).

[111] Maurice Kidron, *Foreign Investments in India* (1965).

[112] B. R. Tomlinson, 'Foreign Private Investment in India 1920–1950', *MAS*, 12, 4 (October 1978) 655–77.

[113] Daniel Thorner, *Investment in Empire. British Railway and Steam Shipping Enterprise in India 1825–1844* (Philadelphia, 1950).

[114] ——————, 'Great Britain and the Development of India's Railways', *JEH*, 11, 4 (Fall 1951) 389–402.

[115] W. J. Macpherson, 'Investment in Indian Railways, 1845–1875', *EHR*, 8, 2 (December 1955) 177–86.

[116] F. Lehmann, 'Great Britain and the Supply of Railway Locomotives to India: A Case Study of Economic Imperialism', *IESHR*, 2, 4 (October 1965) 297–306.

(ii) Foreign Trade and India's Role in the International Economy

Chaudhuri's work has clarified the main features, whilst Saul, De Cecco and Latham emphasise and investigate India's vital role in the international economy of 1870–1914. Farnie provides a useful assessment of India's importance as a market for cotton goods.

[117] K. N. Chaudhuri, 'India's International Economy in the Nineteenth Century: An Historical Survey', *MAS*, 2, 1 (February 1968) 31–50.

[118] —————, *The Economic Development of India under the East India Co. 1814–1858. A Selection of Contemporary Writings* (Cambridge, 1971).

[119] —————, 'India's Foreign Trade and the Cessation of the East India Co.'s Trading Activities 1828–1840', *EHR*, 19, 2 (August 1966) 345–63.

[120] Peter Harnetty, *Imperialism and Free Trade. Lancashire and India in the Mid Nineteenth Century* (Manchester, 1972).

[121] S. B. Saul, *Studies in British Overseas Trade 1870–1914* (Liverpool, 1960).

[122] M. De Cecco, *Money and Empire: The International Gold Standard, 1870–1914* (Oxford, 1974).

[123] A. J. H. Latham, *The International Economy and the Underdeveloped World, 1865–1914* (1978).

[124] —————, 'Merchandise Trade Imbalances and Uneven Economic Development in India and China', *Journal of European Economic History*, 7, 1 (Spring 1978) 33–60.

[125] B. R. Tomlinson, 'India and the British Empire, 1880–1935', *IESHR*, 12, 4 (October 1975) 337–80.

[126] D. A. Farnie, *The English Cotton Industry and the World Market 1815–1896* (Oxford, 1979).

[127] J. D. Tomlinson, 'The First World War and British Cotton Piece Exports to India', *EHR*, 32, 4 (November 1979) 494–506.

[128] Anthony Slaven, 'A Glasgow Firm in the Indian Market: John Lean and Sons, Muslin Weavers', *Business History Review*, 43, 4 (Winter 1969) 496–522.

(iii) The 'Drain' Debate

Besides Chaudhuri's comments attempting to place the 'drain' in perspective [117], Mukerjee provides a modern quantitative assessment of its importance. Ganguli explains the evolution of the concept.

[129] T. Mukerjee, 'The Theory of Economic Drain: The Impact of British Rule on the Indian Economy, 1840–1900', K. E.

Boulding and T. Mukerjee (eds), *Economic Imperialism: A Book of Readings* (Ann Arbor, 1972), pp. 195–212.
[130] B. N. Ganguli, *Dadabhai Naoroji and the Drain Theory* (Calcutta, 1965).

THE STATE AND ECONOMIC DEVELOPMENT

(i) The Intellectual Background to Policy

Whilst the pragmatic basis of policy is now frequently emphasised, the impact of intellectual thought and ideology remains an area of interest and discussion.

[131] Eric Stokes, *The English Utilitarians and India* (Oxford, 1959).
[132] W. J. Barber, *British Economic Thought and India, 1600–1858* (Oxford, 1975).
[133] S. Ambirajan, *Classical Political Economy and British Policy in India* (Cambridge, 1978).

(ii) Government Economic Policy

Lamb provides a valuable overall survey, whilst Sen and Bhattacharya demonstrate that late nineteenth-century policy could not be dogmatically *laissez-faire*. Dewey's is an important article about policy changes during the early twentieth century. Tomlinson discusses the Raj's economic base in its final decades.

[134] Helen B. Lamb, 'The State and Economic Development in India', Simon Kuznets, Wilbert E. Moore and Joseph J. Spengler (eds), *Economic Growth: Brazil, India, Japan* (Durham, N. C. 1955), 464–95.
[135] S. K. Sen, *Studies in Industrial Policy and the Development of India, 1858–1914* (Calcutta, 1964).
[136] S. Bhattacharya, 'Laissez-faire in India', *IESHR*, 2, 1 (January 1965) 1–22.
[137] Clive Dewey, 'The Government of India's "New Industrial Policy", 1900–1925: Formation and Failure', *Economy and Society*, pp. 215–57.

[138] B. R. Tomlinson, *The Political Economy of the Raj 1914–1947. The Economics of Decolonisation in India* (1979).
[139] A. G. Clow, *The State and Industry in India* (Delhi, 1928).
[140] G. G. Jones, 'The State and Economic Development in India, 1890–1947: The Case of Oil', *MAS*, 13, 3 (July 1979) 353–75.
[141] K. N. Reddy, 'Indian Defence Expenditure: 1872–1967', *IESHR*, 7, 4 (December 1970) 467–81.

(iii) Tariff Policy

There are a number of detailed discussions of the major tariff controversies. Dewey's article, however, has wider importance since it explains the forces behind the watershed of the First World War era.

[142] Peter Harnetty, 'The Imperialism of Free Trade: Lancashire and the Indian Cotton Duties, 1859–1862', *EHR*, 18, 2 (August 1965) 333–49.
[143] Ira Klein, 'English Free Traders and Indian Tariffs, 1874–1896', *MAS*, 5, 3 (July 1971) 251–71.
[144] Peter Harnetty, 'The Indian Cotton Duties Controversy, 1894–1896', *English Historical Review*, 77, (October 1962) 684–702.
[145] Clive Dewey, 'The End of the Imperialism of Free Trade: The Eclipse of the Lancashire Lobby and the Concession of Fiscal Autonomy to India', *Imperial Impact*, pp. 35–67.
[146] Ian M. Drummond, 'Indian Tariffs, Cottons and Japanese Competition, 1919–1939', ch. 4 of his *British Economic Policy and the Empire, 1919–1939* (1972).

(iv) Monetary and Financial Issues and Policy

This is an area of recently growing importance in the literature, although many of the fundamental issues had been raised by Keynes. The Tomlinsons (not related!) discuss features of the evolution of policy in the early twentieth century, whilst Rothermund and Adams and West examine the implications of the declining value of the rupee over the late nineteenth century.

[147] J. M. Keynes, *Indian Currency and Finance* (1924).

[148] Dietmar Rothermund, 'The Monetary Policy of British Imperialism', *IESHR*, 7, 1 (March 1970) 91–107.

[149] John Adams and Robert Craig West 'Money, Prices and Economic Development in India, 1861–1895', *JEH*, 39, 1 (March 1979) 55–68.

[150] B. R. Tomlinson, 'Monetary Policy and Economic Development: The Rupee Ratio Question 1921–1927', *Economy and Society*, pp. 197–211.

[151] J. D. Tomlinson, 'The Rupee/Pound Exchange in the 1920s', *IESHR*, 15, 2 (April – June 1978) 133–50.

[152] B. R. Tomlinson, 'Britain and the Indian Currency Crisis, 1930–1932', *EHR*, 32, 1 (February 1979) 88–99.

Index